A Family Journey Through the Bible

An Overview and Devotional for All Ages

MINISTER TONY L. SCOTT

For more information or permissions, please contact the author:
redeemedwriter718@gmail.com
tlmdscott2@gmail.com

Editor: This book was self-edited by the author.

Book Project Management:
Raindrop Creative, Inc. | StartWrite Publish Team
http://www.raindropbrand.com

DEDICATION

This book is lovingly dedicated to my intelligent, inquisitive and helpful 2 ½-year-old grandson, Harrison Scott, and my studious, focused, and soon-to-be big sister, 3-year-old granddaughter, Rumi Land, and to their parents. You are cherished beyond words, and it is my deepest prayer that you come to know Jesus as your personal Lord and Savior, choosing to follow Him with all your heart.

To my beloved wife, Lisa and devoted grandmother, thank you for your steadfast faith and unwavering support. Your love for our family and commitment to God are a constant inspiration.

I also dedicate this book to our future grandchildren, whom we look forward to welcoming with open arms and open hearts. It is my prayer that each of you and our future grandchildren, for generations to come, know the saving grace of Jesus and choose to walk faithfully with Him, just as your grandparents have.

May this book be a guide, a comfort, and a source of encouragement as you seek to grow in your faith and walk with Jesus, My Lord and Savior.

Table of Contents

Preface

The Bible is the world's most important book ever written. It is unique in that it is God's inspired, inerrant and infallible Word. The Bible is *Living* as it tells the story of God's love for His people, from the creation of the world to the promise of a New Heaven and Earth. It's a story that spans generations, cultures, and countless lives transformed by God's grace. Yet, with its vastness and depth, the Bible can feel overwhelming, especially for young readers and families seeking to study it together.

A Family Journey Through the Bible: An Overview and Devotional for All Ages was born from a desire to make the Bible more accessible and engaging for families. This book presents biblical narratives in a way that both children and adults can understand and appreciate. Each chapter highlights key events, characters, and lessons, while devotionals, memory verses, and prayers help deepen your understanding and faith.

Throughout these pages, you will encounter the mighty acts of God, the teachings of Jesus, and the lives transformed by the power of the Holy Spirit. You will see how the Bible's stories are not just ancient texts but living truths that shape our lives today. Whether you are gathered as a family, teaching young hearts, or exploring the Word on your own, this book is designed to guide you on a journey through Scripture.

As you embark on this journey, remember that the Bible is more than just a collection of stories—it's God's message of love, redemption, and hope. My prayer is that this book will inspire you and your family to grow closer to God and one another as you explore His Word together.

Let's journey through the Bible while exploring various biblical narratives and discover God's amazing plan for us all.

Introduction

The Bible is not just an ordinary book—it's the very *Word of God*, an epic journey through time that reveals God's story and His profound love for humanity. From the breathtaking act of creation to the promise of a New Heaven and Earth, the Bible weaves together stories of faith, redemption, struggle, and triumph. It's a story that calls out to every generation, inviting us to understand who God is and what His plan is for our lives.

Yet, reading and understanding the Bible can feel daunting, especially for young readers and families. The language, ancient customs, and complex themes can make it challenging to grasp the full picture. That's why this book exists. *A Family Journey Through the Bible: An Overview and Devotional for All Ages* is crafted to make the Bible's rich story approachable, meaningful, and relevant for everyone.

This book doesn't just retell biblical stories. It helps its readers explore the deeper truths behind each story and see how they connect to God's grand narrative. Each chapter breaks down key events and lessons from the Bible, offering insights that guide readers to understand God's message in a way that resonates with all ages. Additionally, each chapter features a devotional section with memory verses and prayers, encouraging families to reflect on what they've learned and how it applies to their lives.

As you read, you'll encounter stories of courage, faith, sacrifice, and love. You'll see how God worked through ordinary people and how His promises unfolded across generations. You'll also discover how these ancient stories speak directly to our lives today, reminding us that God's love and guidance are as real now as they were in biblical times.

This book is not just for children or adult individual study—it's also for families who want to grow closer to God together. Whether used as a family devotional, a study guide, or a way to introduce children to the Bible, it is designed to bring Scripture to life for everyone.

Let's set out on this family journey through the Bible, discovering how God's Word continues to inspire, challenge, and transform lives. Hear Him through First-Person narration as provided in much of this writing. As you read, discuss, and pray together, may your family be strengthened in faith and drawn closer to God's heart as you give a listening ear and heart to Him.

CHAPTER 1

In the Beginning: God Made Everything Good

Hello, My children. From the Bible, I, your God, Father and your Creator, enjoy speaking to you. I enjoy watching you learn about Me, others and yourself. This book you are reading is not My Bible, but it shares important events and information about the Bible that I want you to know.

From the Book of Genesis

This is what I want you to know about what took place on Earth, beginning with Chapter One of the Bible: In the very beginning, there was nothing. No people. No birds. No animals. No light. No world. Just Me—your God and the Creator of all things good.

Because I wanted a family to love and for them to love Me, I had a big and beautiful plan for planet Earth, which would become my children's home. With My powerful and life-giving words, I said, "Let there be light," and light came shining bright!

I made the sun, the moon, and the stars. I made the oceans and land, the fish and the birds, the animals that walk, and all the plants and trees.

But the most special thing I made was people!

This will be quite amazing to you! I made the body of a man from the earth or dirt of the ground; I called him Adam! Then, after I caused Adam to go into a very deep sleep, I made the woman from Adam's rib! Adam then named the woman Eve.

I created the woman Eve to become Adam's lovely wife. I made them in My image, which means I made them to be like Me, to love, to choose, to care, and with an imagination to create things.

Do you know what else? I am a Spirit Person. That means I don't have the same kind of body that I made for you. When I made Adam and Eve, I made them as spirit beings, too. That means they were made to know Me, love Me, and live with Me forever.

However, just like Adam and Eve, you are also spirit people or spirit beings who have a body of different sizes, shapes, and colors.

I made everyone a little different in their outward appearance so that each person's special uniqueness or differences would make them a wonderful individual to represent My big family or Kingdom on Earth.

Therefore, you, My children, and your parents are just like Adam and Eve; you are also a spirit being, just like Me, but I clothed you and all people with a body. However, all the animals I created on Earth and the angels, who are spirit beings whom I also created, have different bodies than yours!

I, your God and Creator, having clothed you with skin or flesh, is similar to when you wear or clothe yourself with a jacket or shirt and pants to keep your body covered.

And so, it was in the beginning I gave Adam and Eve a body. You and everyone in the whole world are the offspring or children of Adam and Eve. Because I clothed them in a body, when you were born, you also inherited or have bodies just like your fore-parents to clothe you.

Your body is like a jacket, and your invisible spirit is the real you on the inside. I gave you a body so you could live on Earth and show others what I'm like by the way you love, speak, and care for others.

I brought Adam and Eve together as husband and wife, and I told them, "Have children! Fill the Earth with little souls! Teach them to love Me and love one another." This has always been My plan, and it has not changed.

I gave them a beautiful garden to live in called Eden. I walked with them and talked with them. We were together. We were one happy family!

And everything was very good!

What You Should Learn and Remember:

1. You were made by God.
2. You are a spirit being, just like God is Spirit.
3. You live in a body that God gave you to show His love on Earth.
4. You were made to love God and others.
5. God made families to be filled with love and His goodness.

Memory Verses:

A. "In the beginning, God created the Heavens and the Earth." — Genesis 1:1

B. "God is Spirit, and those who worship Him must worship in spirit and truth." —John 4:24

C. "So, God created man in His own image… male and female He created them." —Genesis 1:27

D. "Then the Lord God formed the man from the dust of the ground and breathed into his nostrils the breath of life, and the man became a living soul." —Genesis 2:7

E. "God saw all that He had made, and it was very good." —Genesis 1:31

Let's Talk:

1. What does it mean that you are a spirit being made in God's image?

2. How can you use your body to show God's love today?

Prayer:

Dear LORD,

Thank You for making me a spirit being, just like You.
Thank You for giving me a body to live in and to show Your love.
Help me remember that I belong to You and that I am made to love You and others.
Thank You for making everything good.
In Jesus' name, Amen.

CHAPTER 2

A Sad Choice: A Sneaky Snake and a Big Promise

From the Book of Genesis

Hello, My children. This is what I want you to know in Chapter Two.

Once upon a time, everything was perfect. Yes, I made everything perfect. Adam and Eve walked with Me in their beautiful garden home. There were no lies. No sadness. No sickness. No death. Just joy, peace, and love!

However, something very sad and unfortunate then happened.

There was another creature that was in the garden. It was a harmless, beautiful creature called a snake—one of the many peaceful and gentle animals I had made. But on this day, something terrible happened to My amazing creature.

Satan, a rebellious and evil spirit being who had once been one of My good angels, whose name was then called Lucifer, becoming a bad or disobedient angel, used the snake to trick or deceive Eve.

This is why Earth experiences very severe or extreme storms, such as hurricanes, tornadoes, flooding, and other bad natural events, so they are called. It was like a big crack that appeared in the beautiful world I had made.

After they disobeyed me, suddenly, Adam and Eve felt shame and fear!

They understood immediately that they had done a very bad thing by not listening to Me, their loving Daddy and God. They then tried to hide from Me! But you can't hide from your Daddy, who loves you and knows everything that is happening everywhere and at all times!

Because I am God, I know everything, and I see everything. There are some things I see and hear that make Me very happy! Then, there are things that I see and hear that make Me very sad.

Because I am holy or perfect, meaning I can do no wrong because I am loving and just, I had to give Adam and Eve and the serpent consequences or punishment for not listening to Me!

So I told the serpent, also known as Satan, that he would have to crawl on his belly and eat dust from the ground.

I told Eve that mothers will experience pain during childbirth as a reminder of her disobedience!

I told Adam the ground would be hard to work on. That work for Adam would be difficult as he worked in the fields!

But the saddest part. I had to send Adam and Eve away from the garden, the home that we shared together. They could no longer walk or be one with Me in the same way.

The closeness we had was broken; we became distant or far apart because of their sin of disobedience; I was so hurt because My children did not listen to me!

They chose not to follow My instructions, which would have kept them safe and close to Me, along with My loving guidance and protection.

Little children, I hope that you are listening to your parents. They are listening to Me. I am so proud of your parents because they are listening to Me. And I am also proud of you because you are listening to your parents!

When Adam and Eve disobeyed Me, I was so sad! But I did not stop loving them; I love them very much! Yes, I still loved them, and I love you, too, even when you make mistakes.

I know that no one is perfect like Me. Therefore, I understand that My children will sometimes make mistakes or make bad choices.

However, I always want you to think about any bad choices you may make. I want you to learn from your mistakes. But I also want you to pray to Me by saying that you are sorry and then ask Me to help you make better choices and to do better.

I just love helping you and seeing all of My children learn and grow as you listen to your parents and study your Bibles!

Before Adam and Eve left the garden, I made clothes for them to cover their shame or nakedness. I showed My love and care for them. But I also gave them a promise—the most important promise ever!

I told them and the wicked-rebellious serpent or Satan, "One day, the child of a woman will come. He will crush the serpent's head."

That means this *child* was going to grow up and defeat the serpent, who is also called Satan. But he, this wicked and evil spirit person—Satan was going to strike or hurt the *child* when he grew up.

But in the end, the adult child is going to destroy or put away forever all evil or bad things, including Satan, who is very wicked and extremely bad! Then all of My children will be happy and shout for joy!

That promised child is speaking about My Unique—One of a Kind Son, Jesus!

One day, Jesus would come, and He has already come into the world to war against sin, death and Satan. And He has won the battle of **Good** over evil! This is what is called spiritual warfare.

And not the ugly, mean, and wrong fighting that people do to hurt and kill each other. However, such things do occur because of the influence of spiritual evil.

People say bad things and fight each other because of sin or the meanness that we can sometimes feel inside of us. But I want people to love each other, not to be mean, fight, and hate others.

One day, Jesus will make all things right! But He has already made the way for My children like you to come back to Me so that you may be returned to My family and live with Me forever in My kingdom. Doesn't that sound exciting?!

However, because I love you and My other children so much, one day, I am going to fix this broken world and make everything new!

Do you remember that I told you that Satan came into My beautiful garden called Eden? While there, he influenced, inhabited, or entered the body of a creature that we call a serpent or snake.

He did this so that he could lie to and trick Eve. He made her think that disobeying Me would be okay. What a horrible and mean thing to do!

Then Adam disobeyed Me, too, and that's when sin entered the world, and things began to get very bad on Earth and within the hearts of all people. This is what I mean when I say the Earth and people are broken.

Not every person is the same. Some people are more bad and evil or broken than others. Even little children can do bad things, such as being untruthful, not listening to their parents, hitting others, and taking things that don't belong to them.

I hope you don't do this. Such things make Me very sad. Such behavior or things are sinful or wrong!

Sin or being sinful is doing something that goes against My love and truth. Sin separates people from Me because I am Holy or Perfect in all of My ways. This means that no sin or sinful ways are in Me, unlike My people who I love.

Just as the fallen angels, neither can adult people or older individuals who do not feel remorse for their wrong actions or sinful behavior be one with Me or a part of My loving family.

This is why everyone needs Jesus, so you can be forgiven for your sins or wrong behavior. When you are sad about doing something wrong or bad. I, your God, will lovingly forgive you if you ask Me to.

I am willing to forgive you because I love you so very much (Luke 13:3; John 3:16; Acts 3:19)!

Now, My child, let Me tell you something more about how I made people, including you. I made you in My image so that you may be like Me in doing good and loving others.

Remember that I told you that I am a Spirit-Being or Spirit Person? Well, you are a spirit being or spirit person, just like Me, your Creator and Father. However, you as a human being were created by Me, who has always existed. I was not made or created like you are.

But look at yourself; I gave you something special—I clothed your spirit that you cannot see, with a body covered or made of skin, similarly to when you put on your clothes. You can see your clothing just like you can see your body.

But you can't see your invisible spirit, just like you cannot see the air you breathe or the wind that blows and makes tree leaves move.

Do you have a jacket and shirt and pants? When you put those on, your real self or body and spirit are either inside you or under your clothing, right? Yes!

And so, you are a spirit being clothed with either a girl's body or a boy's body! I made Adam as a man. And I created Eve to be a woman.

I created only two bodies or two genders for My people. I created both male and female bodies. Which body do you have? You were born either as a boy or a girl; this is how I made you. You have been wonderfully made by Me (Psalm 139:14)!

And so, your body is something like your clothes that cover you; it helps you live on Earth, to feel and taste things, to move, and to do good things for others if you choose to. I hope you will. This is what I want you to do: help others and always be kind and loving.

Once again, your spirit is the real you, just like I am a Spirit Person and your God! One day, I will give you a new body that is whole and unbroken. You, My child, and everyone who obeys Me and My Son Jesus will no longer get sick or die (Revelation 21:4). Isn't that great?!

When I covered you with skin and made you come alive, you became a living soul. Wow! Isn't that incredible?! You are truly special to Me! I love you so much!

I have also given you an awesome mind to think with and to be creative, just like Me, your Creator and Daddy. You also have feelings and emotions so that you may care for and love others, just as I do.

And so, it is because of your spirit, who you really are, that you are enabled by the Holy Spirit to be one with Me and to be a part of My loving spiritual family or Kingdom.

The Holy Spirit provides the only way for you to be born again, to unite with Me and become a part of My family. Believing in Jesus as my Unique Son has everything to do with this happening!

I will tell you how this happens in a little while. Just keep reading and listening... Okay?

Here's something else I want you to think about: Have you ever played with a balloon? Have you ever blown air into your balloon or seen your mom or dad blow one up? The balloon is something you can see and touch. Is that correct? It's made of a material—rubber.

Just like your body, which is made of a different material or substance, and not rubber, that is of a different kind of substance or matter. But when you blow air into your balloon, something happens—the balloon fills up and takes on different and beautiful shapes and sizes!

The air that gives the balloon different shapes and sizes is kind of like your spirit that is in your body. You can't see your spirit or anyone else's spirit, but it's what helps to give form or shape and life to your body.

The air breathed into the balloon is necessary for the balloon to take on a beautiful and wonderful shape. And so, it is with you being a spirit; your spirit makes your body come to life with its beautiful shapes, sizes and colors!

Your spirit that I created in My image and gave life to it or you, which is kind of like air or similar to air that provides life to all creatures. However, Me creating you as a spirit being is far greater and more important to Me than a balloon and all other living things.

You are, in fact, My children!

It is you, as a spiritual person, that gives your physical body life! Because of these two aspects of who you are and being joined together by Me, you have become a living soul or a human being!

Therefore, you, as a spirit person, are now able the join with Me, your Dad, who is the Great Supreme Spirit Person! It is because of Me that you are alive, moving, and breathing in the physical realm called Earth (Acts 17:28).

Can you now understand why I love you so much? Yes, it's because I created you! You are so special to Me; you are My very own children! I am your Heavenly Father. This also means that you can call Me Daddy!

I also have a name, just like you do. My name is Yahweh; sometimes, people call Me Jehovah. My Unique Son's name is Jesus.

What is your name? I like your name _____.

As your Father and Creator, I am the One who gives the Life-giving breath or spirit to your physical body. It is My Essence or Breath that gives you life. Only people, such as yourself, are made in my image. That's what makes you and all people so very special to Me!

Even though you can't see the air in the balloon, just like you cannot see Me with your eyes. Nevertheless, I am alive, and I am the God who made your soul come alive. I did this by breathing My Life-giving or Empowering breath into your earthly or physical body.

That's how I made Adam and Eve come alive and everyone born after them. It is My air or breath that you breathe.

However, it is the Empowering Holy Spirit that will enter your body and become one with your soul. His Power enables you to be born again! And, therefore, one with Me so that you may live with Me forever and ever! Then you will be able to see Me in a wonderful way!

But, do you remember that one day when Adam and Eve were in the garden and disobeyed Me? Well, their actions caused their spirits or souls to become sinful or bad and the world to become broken. Because of what they did, I, their Eternal Life-giving Spirit, had to depart from them.

Therefore, My children could no longer walk with Me in the same way they once did. The Holy or Life-giving Spirit was no longer in or connected to them. They still breathed My air, which provided life to their bodies.

But sadly, I could no longer be with Adam and Eve or spiritually one with them or connected to My children. They had become unholy or defiled because of their sin of disobedience.

I, therefore, and with great sadness, had to send them out of the garden I had made for them. That was the place where they worshiped Me, and we would have fun and enjoy one another as a family!

As time moved on, one day, Adam and his wife Eve had children, and their first two sons were named Cain and Abel. When Cain grew up, he worked in the fields, and when Abel grew up, he took care of sheep.

One day, when they were older, both of them brought their gift or sacrifice to Me to show that they honored or respected Me and that they loved Me.

This is what they were instructed or taught to do by their parents, as I had also instructed their parents. They were being obedient by doing this.

However, it was Abel who gave his very best gift or sacrifice before Me. His heart or thoughts towards Me were right or good. He had listened to Me more carefully than his brother Cain. Abel knew exactly what I required or wanted from him. Therefore, he wanted to honor and please Me.

Abel, on the other hand, knew what right and wrong were, as I had told or instructed him and his brother according to their parents' teachings about Me.

They both knew what I desired or required from them so that they could show or demonstrate love, obedience, respect, or reverence towards Me.

Nevertheless, Cain did not listen to Me as he should have. Therefore, I lovingly accepted Abel, his brother's gift, but I had to lovingly reject or disapprove of Cain's sacrifice. What you should understand is that their gift or sacrifice was not only for Me.

Their sacrifice also was a way for them to recognize and accept that they were sinful. With their sacrifice, they acknowledge that they were broken people. And that they were in need of My help to be forgiven of their sins and to be once again accepted by Me.

Sadly, Cain's heart was not toward doing good or what was right in My sight. Tragically, Cain became very angry because I did not accept his sacrifice or offering to Me!

I warned Cain how anger could cause him to do bad things! I said to Cain, "Sin," or something bad, is "crouching at your door" or in his heart, and it wants you to do bad things in order to control you.

But you must not do the bad things, I said to him. Instead, choose to do what is right or good, what will make Me proud and happy towards you. But Cain didn't listen to Me!

He became so angry and jealous of his brother Abel that he did an extremely troublesome and bad thing! Cain killed his own brother, Abel! This was just awful! Everyone was so sad, and they were crying! That was the first time someone took the life of another person!

It made Me—their Daddy and God very sad. Cain's actions showed how dangerous and hurtful sin had become. This is what sin can do to anyone if you do not love Me and listen to your God.

As more and more people were born, sin kept growing or spreading in the world, and the things people did became worse and worse! People didn't want to listen to Me. They only wanted to do what was evil in their hearts.

Some people are just like them today. Make sure you don't listen to them! Always listen to your parents and Me.

However, sometime later, something even more terrible or sinister happened! (See Genesis 6:1-4; 2 Peter 2:4,5; Jude 1:6,7).

This is what occurred: Some of the wicked angels, such ones were those who followed Satan in his rebellion against Me, also came down to the Earth. They chose to leave their heavenly home or the unseen realm that I had assigned for them.

These rebellious angels would not obey or listen to Me! They came to Earth to mislead My people! The men I made on Earth listened to these wicked angels. These angels were, therefore, allowed or permitted to do strange, harmful or sinful things with women!

What they did was to have unnatural relationships—something like marriages with women. This was not as I intended, not at all! Yes, the fallen angels came to the Earth, your world and did very wicked things and misled My children!

These wicked-rebellious angels were able to take on or have bodies very similar to yours, and they married My female human beings; together, they had babies who were not made in My image!

These strange or unnatural offspring or children that came from these marriages or unions—angels marrying earth-born women were not part of my plan! I was so hurt and troubled that this happened!

And so it was, these unusual beings who were born and children that grew up were not made in My image like you are. They were a different kind of creature. They were very corrupt; they were wicked or evil all of the time, just like the fallen angels who were their dads.

Now, all of the people were doing bad things all the time, and everywhere they went! This was a terrible, terrible thing that happened! The fallen angels and My people had stopped listening to Me, their God and Creator.

These exceedingly wicked angels' unusual children, who were not like you or your Mommy and Daddy and everybody else, when they died, they are what I now call demons or foul and unclean spirit beings!

Because of the evil humans and the wicked angels' bad ways, their wickedness or the bad things they did spread like fire all over the world! This was not good!

Violence by people and mean, and hurtful things were taking place everywhere, and My heart was deeply disturbed and troubled! I knew that something had to be done!

But even though I was going to judge the world to bring a stop to these horrible things, I still loved My people! Satan and the other wicked angels were not going to stop the plans that I had for My people and the world!

Before I created the world, I knew that this was going to happen. However, you should know that I am always in control, even though I permit bad things to happen.

Remember, I told you, because of sin, that the world and people are broken; this is why bad things are always happening on Earth or in this world. But one day, I will bring a complete end to all the evil and sadness that you see and experience. I promise!

Nevertheless, I still wanted a family on Earth who would love Me, worship Me, serve Me, and show the world what I am like… A God of love, a Daddy who also wants His children to really try to do the right things with My help.

These will be people or My true children and family who do not enjoy doing bad things or committing sin. But rather, My children who will obey Me and who want to make Me happy by showing and teaching the world just how much I love them.

While all the evil was happening everywhere in the world, there was one man who listened to Me. His name was Noah. While the world was full of disobedience, darkness or great evil, Noah walked with Me and listened to Me.

Noah was an obedient child of mine. He taught his family to obey Me too. I saw Noah's good heart and good intentions, and I was pleased. I was so proud of him and happy because he listened to My teachings and instructions.

So I told Noah, "Build a big boat, an ark." I said to him, "I will bring a great flood, a lot of rain and water to wash the Earth clean of sinful or bad and disobedient people, but I will save you and your family."

Noah obeyed Me, even when the world laughed at him. He trusted Me, and he listened to his God and Daddy. When the ark—the very huge boat was finished, Noah brought in his family, and I brought in two of every kind of animal: cows, horses, deer, rabbits and everything.

Then I shut the door to the huge boat. The rain came down! A lot of rain fell down upon Earth for forty days and nights, and the whole world flooded.

Everything that breathed or that was living outside the Ark was gone or destroyed by the water and great flood! Sin had brought great sadness and My judgment. But Noah and his family were kept safe by Me because they believed in Me and obeyed their God.

I saved Noah and his family because I still wanted a family on Earth. I wanted a people who would worship Me, love Me, and live for Me. I wanted a people who would care for one another and take care of the beautiful Earth I had made for them.

I wanted people, or My true children, who would be My imagers—who would reflect who I am. So, I gave the world a new start through Noah and his family.

When the water finally dried up, I made a promise to Noah and to every person after him. I placed a rainbow in the sky. It was My sign of love, mercy, and hope. I said, "I will never again destroy the earth with a flood."

What You Should Learn and Remember:

1. God is a Spirit who has always existed. He is your loving Creator.
2. Jesus is Unique because He was not made. He also eternally exists, just like God, His Father.
3. You are a spirit being clothed in a body, just like a balloon holds invisible air to come alive as it takes shape. But not really alive like boys and girls and other people who have God's breath in them.
4. God made the angels, but some disobeyed and, like Satan, became the enemy of God and of His people.
5. Sin started with Adam and Eve, and it grew worse through Cain and others.
6. Sin makes God sad because it hurts people and separates them from His love.
7. God is Holy and must judge sin, but He is also loving and wants to save people.
8. God saved Noah because Noah had faith and obeyed and because God still wanted a family to love and care for on Earth.

Memory Verses:

A. "God is Spirit, and those who worship Him must worship in spirit and in truth." —John 4:24
B. "Sin is crouching at your door; it desires to have you, but you must rule over it." —Genesis 4:7
C. "Cain attacked his brother Abel and killed him." —Genesis 4:8
D. "The Lord saw how great the wickedness of the human race had become... and His heart was deeply troubled." —Genesis 6:5-6
E. "But Noah found grace in the eyes of the Lord." —Genesis 6:8

F. "By faith, Noah... built an ark to save his family." —Hebrews 11:7

G. "I have set My rainbow in the clouds, and it will be the sign of the covenant between Me and Earth." —Genesis 9:13

Let's Talk:

1. Why do you think Noah obeyed God even when others didn't?
2. What does the rainbow remind us about God's love and promises?
3. What can you do when you feel angry or tempted to do wrong?
4. What makes your spirit alive inside your body?

Prayer:

Dear Daddy,

Thank You for making me a spirit-being like You.
Thank You for giving me a body, like clothes for my spirit, so I can live on Earth as a living soul. Thank You for Your breath of life, like air in a balloon.
Help me say "yes" to You and "no" to sin.
Help me be like Noah—trusting, loving, and listening to You always.
Thank You for rainbows, for new beginnings, and for Your love that never ends.
In Jesus' name, Amen.

CHAPTER 4
A Promise and a Blessing

From the Book of Genesis

Hello, My sons and daughters. This is what I want you to know in Chapter Four.

I am your God. I am Good, Holy, and True.
I made you. I love you. I want you to know Me.
I want to be your heavenly Father, and I want you to become My children.

Do you remember the story of the flood? The world had become very wicked! People and angels were doing evil things! Even some angels, who were supposed to remain in heaven, did not obey Me. They came to Earth and had strange and forbidden relationships with the daughters of men.

This made the world full of terrible sins and great darkness! So, I sent a global flood to wash away all the evil caused by the wicked people and angels. However, I kept Noah and his family safe because Noah obeyed Me.

I used the flood to clean the world of sin and the disobedient people and fallen angels. Then, I gave the world **a new beginning.** However, I knew that my people would still struggle with sin and disobey Me.

I also wanted the people to see that they really had a horrible sin problem. And that without listening to Me, they would create all kinds of problems for themselves; things that saddened Me and things I did not like!

Nevertheless, I already knew the people would continue to fail and disappoint Me. Therefore, I had a plan even before I created the world.

My plan to fix the world and save people would rest in and be fulfilled through My Son Jesus when He comes into the world to die for the sins of humanity. And at His Second Coming to restore His Kingdom on Earth!

You will learn more about Him as you continue to read this book and listen to My teachings.

After the flood, Noah's sons and daughters had children, and their children had more children. Soon, Earth began to fill with people again. But many people still didn't want to follow Me.

They tried to make their own way or do what they wanted to do without following or listening to Me. They even tried to build a tall tower up to the sky, called the Tower of Babel, thinking they could find their own god.

But that was not My plan! And their bad plan would have major consequences!

So, I stopped their self-sufficient building project and scattered them across Earth, giving them different languages to speak. They were all confused by the miracle I had caused.

However, I still had a plan to bless the world or help all the people who would listen to Me, not relying on their own efforts but instead doing what I instructed them to do.

I still wanted a family—people who would listen to Me, love Me, and who would one day live with Me forever. So, I chose a man named Abram. Later, I changed his name to Abraham. His name means he would become the father of many nations or people.

Abraham listened to Me. I said, "Abraham, leave your home and follow Me. I will give you a new land. I will make your family into a great nation. And through your family, I will bless the whole world."

Abraham believed Me. He obeyed Me. Even when he didn't understand everything, he trusted Me. That made Me so happy!

I gave Abraham a special promise. I told him he would have a son, even though he was very old. His wife Sarah was also very old, but nothing is too hard for Me!

And guess what? I kept My promise. I always keep My promise. Sarah had a baby boy. His name was Isaac. Isaac had a son named Jacob. And Jacob had twelve sons! This big family became the beginning of My special people—the people of Israel!

I wanted Abraham's family to be a light or to be truth-tellers to the other people on Earth. I love and care for everyone! Therefore, I want everyone to learn the truth about Me. And then choose to obey Me, thereby being led by My words of truth.

You see, I wanted people to show others all over the world how to truly love and honor Me. It is My loving desire for My people on Earth to obey Me, worship Me, and walk in My ways that lead to Eternal Life!

It would be through Abraham's family I was going to send someone very, very special—My Unique Son, Jesus, who would save the world from sin. He is then going to give Me, His Father's children, Eternal Life!

This means that you and all others will not have to fear dying anymore or the consequences of sin! Here is why death is no longer to be feared: My children, when your bodies die and are buried or returned to the earth, your spirits are really just asleep and returned to be with Me!

And when you are awakened, My sons and daughters are going to be with Me in paradise always! Then, I am going to give my daughters and sons new bodies that will live forever!

I am excited that one day soon, My sons and daughters will be returning home to be with Me always! You should also be excited; this is great news!

Listen to Me carefully; everyone you love who loves my **Special Son Jesus** will also be there with you and Me. We will be one big happy family!

What You Should Learn and Remember:

1. God used the flood to clean the broken world from the great evil within sinful or disobedient people and angels who lived in the world.
2. God gave the world a new start with Noah's family.
3. People still sinned, but God had a plan.
4. God chose Abraham to be the father of a new family on Earth.

5. Abraham trusted God, and God kept His promise.
6. God blesses those who follow and obey Him.

Memory Verses:

A. "I will bless you… and you will be a blessing." —Genesis 12:2
B. "Abraham believed God." —Romans 4:3
C. "Nothing is too hard for the Lord." —Genesis 18:14

Let's Talk:

1. Why did God choose Abraham?
2. What does it mean to trust and obey God?
3. How can you be a blessing to others?

Prayer:

Dear God,

Thank You for loving us, even when the world is full of sin.
Thank You for giving the world a fresh start with Noah's family.
Thank You for choosing Abraham to bless the world.
Help me to trust You and follow You every day.
I want to be part of Your family.
I love You, my Father.
In Jesus' name, I pray. Amen.

CHAPTER 5

The Exodus: God Delivers His People

Hello, My beloved family. Here's what I want you to learn in Chapter Five.

I am the God who always remembers and fulfills My promises.
I am the God who hears My children when they cry.
I am the God who comes to rescue and save.

From the Book of Exodus

There was a boy named Joseph; he was Abraham's great-grandson. He was one of the sons of Jacob, also called Israel. Jacob was Abraham's grandson. Jacob's father was called Isaac; Isaac was the son of Abraham.

I made a promise to Abraham that he would become great! Abraham became great, and he remains great because of his faith in Me. But also because Jesus, your Lord and Savior, came through his family.

Joseph also trusted or had faith in Me, even when hard and bad things happened. Everybody experiences hard or difficult times. But you should always trust Me even when things get hard or are bad in the world.

My child, I may not change your situation. But I still love you no matter what! Remember, the world that you currently live in is broken or flawed. Therefore, I want you to always remember that one day, you will live with Me forever in your new world!

Keep reminding yourself that the troubles of this world will not last always!

Joseph experienced a sad and horrible thing; he was taken or stolen from his family by his own brothers. He was then sold and carried far away to another country called Egypt, but I had a plan to save or rescue him and many others as well.

Joseph, whom I saved and raised up to become a great leader, learned to trust and obey Me. I enabled Joseph with wisdom and the ability to interpret dreams. Because of Joseph's giftings, he would save the people of Egypt from a great famine—a time when no food would grow.

That was a hard time for many people whom I love. However, remember that I always have a plan!

Sometimes, you may not understand My plan or why I allow certain things, or even bad things, to happen. But I want you to always trust Me! Always believe in your eternal hope that comes through My Son Jesus!

One day, I am going to put a final stop to all evil and bad people. Will you trust me? I sure hope so. This will make Me extremely happy and proud, and I will be so pleased with you!

Because of Joseph, Pharaoh, who was the king of Egypt, gave Joseph's whole family a place to live in Egypt and food. Joseph's family had come to Egypt to find food because of the famine.

But Joseph would also be reunited with his family once again. This became a time for rejoicing! Everyone was so happy and thankful to Me!

Joseph's family was treated kindly and had food and land. But years passed. Joseph died, and so did Pharaoh. New kings came, and they did not remember Joseph or how he had helped the Egyptian people become wealthy.

And they—the Egyptian leaders were afraid of My people because they had grown into a great big family, a whole nation! This only began to fulfill the promise that I had made to Abraham, that he would become the father of many nations and people. See how I keep my promises?

So the new Pharaoh or king made My people into slaves. This was awful! People should not be treated like this! I was so disappointed! But remember, I always have a great plan, and it includes your well-being!

Pharaoh forced them to work very hard! He was mean and cruel to My people, Israel! He even tried to kill the baby boys so they would not grow up strong by listening to Me and honoring their God and Father. This was a very bad and wicked thing that Pharaoh attempted to do!

Pharaoh's heart was hard or against Me! He did know this, but he was also being led by spiritual evil and Satan. You see, Satan knew that the Messiah, My *Special* Son, would be born through the family of Israel.

Therefore, he was using Pharaoh to try to stop the *Child* from being born, who was going to crush or destroy him. But I had a plan. I always have a plan!

I chose a baby boy named Moses, who would grow up to become a leader and deliverer for My people. Moses' life and leadership were a mirror or foreshadowing of what Jesus would later do. I told you I always have a plan!

Even though Pharaoh wanted to destroy the Israelite baby boys, I kept Moses safe. He was placed in a small basket by his sister and mother, which was left to float on the river because they trusted Me and knew he would be saved.

Just as Noah had a boat that I told him to build, which floated on the water so that I could save him and his family.

In like manner, I also saved Moses and rescued him from his basket that floated on the river so that Moses, by My help, would save or deliver My people from Egyptian bondage.

Pharaoh's daughter's servant girl heard the baby crying. She then found Moses in the basket and took him to her. Pharaoh's daughter then raised the baby in the palace as her own son. This was also a part of My great plan or strategy!

Yet, when Moses grew up, he saw how terrible My people and his family, the Israelites, were being treated by the corrupt Egyptian leaders. This serves as a mirror of how Satan and sin have sinful people in bondage. As a result of this bondage, My people are also oppressed!

However, Moses, My appointed leader, did a bad thing! He did not listen to Me; he became angry and decided to do things his own way. Noah, just like Cain, killed someone! It was one of the bad guards who was hurting one of My people and Moses' fellow men, an Israelite brother.

After Moses did this, he became afraid because others knew what he had done. Therefore, he ran away to the desert. But one day, I met with Moses and talked to him through a burning bush! This was a miracle for Moses to see how Mighty and Powerful *I am*!

Moses could not believe what he was seeing! I said, "Moses, I want you to go back to Pharaoh and tell him to let My people go." Moses was afraid! He said, "I'm not strong. I can't talk well." But I said, "I will be with you."

You see, I am always with My children, no matter how hard or how bad things are. I then chose Aaron, Moses' older brother, to help him. I also used Moses' sister, Miriam—she would sing and help the people worship Me once they were free from Egyptian bondage or enslavement.

I remind you that all people are enslaved to sin. But the Good News is that Jesus sets you free just like I used Moses to set My people free! But when Jesus sets you free from the bondage of sin, He also helps you to live good or righteous lives before Me, your God and Father.

Do you thank Jesus for what He has done? I really love My Unique Son, Jesus! How about you?

Now listen carefully, My beloved children. You must understand and always keep in your mind this spiritual truth. This wasn't just a battle between Moses and Pharaoh. As I've mentioned, there was something else happening that you couldn't see with your eyes.

Satan, who is a spirit being and who is also called the Devil—that fallen angel we've talked about—was trying to stop My plan. He didn't want My promise to Abraham to come true. He didn't want My people to be free.

Satan was trying to stop Jesus from being born! Do you remember the child whom I promised was going to strike the serpent's or Satan's head? Well, that child is Jesus!

Later, I will discuss Jesus' birth, when He, the incarnate God, came into the world. And how Jesus defeated Satan and everything harmful and evil!

You see, I always win! I am Victorious! I am the Almighty and Powerful God!

Sometimes, it does not look like it. But trust Me, I am winning, and I've already won! And you are also a winner or victorious because you are choosing to listen to Me and follow My son Jesus.

You see, Jesus' birth, death, and coming alive again have proven that we all have won!

As for letting My people, Israel, go, Pharaoh said "No!" many times. So, I showed him My Power!

I sent signs called plagues: frogs, flies, darkness, sickness, and even hail to judge or punish Pharaoh. But Pharaoh's heart was hard and full of pride! He would not listen to Me and My servant Moses.

Then came the last sign, or My punishment of Pharaoh and the Egyptian people!... My destroying or death angel!

I told My people to put the blood of a lamb on their doors; this was another mirror or foreshadowing pointing to the shed blood of Jesus. My Son Jesus' blood also protects My children from death or the consequences of sin.

Jesus is also called the sinless and **Perfect Lamb of God,** who takes away the sins of the world. And who took upon His body your punishment for sin! This is Good News!

When My destroying angel came to Egypt to stop the bad king and his leader's rebellion, the death angel passed over My people's houses and kept them safe because of the blood of the lamb.

You see, this is just what Jesus has done! His sacrifice and blood give you Salvation and keep you eternally safe, no matter what bad things you experience or that may happen to you while you live in this broken world.

This is Good News! Your eternal Salvation! Whereby you will live with Jesus forever!

However, the Egyptian families were not kept safe. Subsequently, their oldest sons died when the death angel came because Pharaoh, who tried to destroy My sons, would not obey Me! That night, Pharaoh finally said, "Go!" And My people left Egypt.

When My people left Egypt, I led them with a large cloud by day and a bright fire by night! This was how they knew where to go. This was another of the many miracles that I performed. You see, My people were actually being led by God the Holy Spirit; He was in the cloud and the fire.

What I want you to understand is that when you choose to follow Me, it is the Holy Spirit who has led you to Me, and it is He who leads you when you listen to Me.

But Pharaoh did a bad thing; he did not listen to Me. He rebelled again and changed his mind and chased My people with his army! My people came to the Red Sea, and they were so afraid! But I made a way!... I opened the sea by My Mighty Power!

My people, Israel, walked through the raised sea walls on dry ground. This was also an awesome miracle, once again showing the world My Mighty Power!

But when Pharaoh's army tried to follow My people, I caused the sea walls to crash back down and stopped them! They all died because they would not listen to Me, their God and Creator.

Sadly, I had to punish them because they always remained rebellious and disobedient! Their hearts were hard, and their minds were made up to rebel against Me; this is why they were destroyed.

But I saved Israel, My chosen people, and many others who chose to follow Me, Israel's God. Moses sang a song of joy! Miriam danced and sang with the women! They praised Me for being their Deliverer and Mighty God!

As My people traveled through the desert or wilderness, even when they didn't always listen or were afraid, I still helped them because of the promise I made to Abraham. These were My chosen people—the Israelites, also called Jews.

They were the people of my promise to Abraham because of his faith in Me. Therefore, I had and still have a special plan for Israel or the Jewish people. Even though, as a nation, they did not and currently do not listen to or accept Jesus as their King.

While the Jewish people traveled in the wilderness, I provided them with special food from heaven, called Manna, and water to drink that came from a rock. I wanted them to know that **I Am** the only true God.

I gave them My rules so they would know how to live and obey Me. Will you listen to Me and obey My teaching as provided in the Bible? I told My people, Israel, to be kind, to love Me, and to love one another.

Moses grew older and died. But I had picked a new leader named Joshua to lead My children. He would lead My people to the land I had promised long ago to Abraham and his descendants.

My strategy was still moving forward. My plan is always moving forward, no matter how bad things get or how mean people may become.

What You Should Learn and Remember:

1. God always remembers and keeps His promises.
2. God hears us when we pray, and He knows when we are hurting.
3. God uses people, even those who are fearful, like Moses, to accomplish great things. Will you let God use you?
4. Pharaoh's pride and the Devil's tricks couldn't stop God's plan.
5. God saves His people with great power and great love.

Memory Verses:

A. "By faith Moses' parents hid him for three months." —Hebrews 11:23
B. "By faith, the people passed through the Red Sea as on dry land." —Hebrews 11:29

C. "Let My people go!" —Exodus 8:1
D. "The Lord will fight for you; you need only to be still." —Exodus 14:14

Let's Talk:

1. How did Joseph help bring his family to Egypt?
2. Why did Pharaoh make God's people slaves?
3. What did Moses do when God called him?
4. What do we learn about God's Power and love?

Prayer:

Dear God,

Thank You for never forgetting Your promises.
Thank You for hearing our cries and coming to help.
Help me to be brave like Moses and trust You like Joshua.
Even when I'm scared, or things feel too big,
Help me remember You are stronger than anything.
Thank You for saving us and loving us.
In Jesus' name, Amen.

CHAPTER 6

The Ten Commandments:
God Gives His Law

(Scripture References: Exodus 19–20; Deuteronomy 5; Galatians 3:24)

Hello, My child. It is always good for Me to talk to you and for you to follow My instructions. This is what I want you to know from Chapter Six.

I am the God who saves and speaks.
I am holy, and I want you to know how to live in love and truth.
I have given you My Word to teach you because I love you.
I give My Law to show you what is right and acceptable.

Do you remember how I brought My people, the Israelites, out of Egypt? I rescued them from Pharaoh and from slavery. I opened the Red Sea and led them through it safely.

Now, My people, who are also called Hebrews, were in the wilderness, traveling to the land I had promised them for their home.

But before they arrived, I wanted to teach them how to live as My special or chosen people. So, I brought My people, Israel, to a large mountain called Mount Sinai. I told Moses, whom I made leader of My people Israel, to "Come up the mountain. I will speak with you."

The people stayed at the bottom, and I came down to the mountain in a cloud with thunder and lightning. There was a loud trumpet sound, and the mountain shook! The people were scared, and they stood far away!

They had said to Moses, "You speak to us. Don't let God speak to us, or we will die!" Many of the people feared Me because they understood that I was a Holy, Righteous and Just God who would and even one day will punish all wrongdoers who reject Me and My Son Jesus.

Because My people, Israel, hearts, were not righteous or good enough to stand before Me, sadly, they were afraid of My justice and Me, their loving God.

However, what you should also understand. It's very important that you get this:

It is because of My Unique Son Jesus, who is the Lamb of God and who gave Himself as a sacrifice and died for your sins and the sins of the world. And Who is now alive forever as the King of kings.

This, My Son Jesus, who is now in heaven with Me, has sent God the Holy Spirit to dwell in you and to be with you all of the time!

The Holy Spirit has come into the world to give you New Life, to lead you, to teach you My ways and to remind you of My unceasing love for you, but also of My righteous justice!

Because of My love for you, now God the Holy Spirit can and does dwell or live in the soul of all of My children, no matter their sinful past or wherever they may live in the whole world.

My true children are those who have repented or turned from living a life of sin. Those who listen to Jesus and what We have to say, which is written in the Bible.

Such are those who are My true sons and daughters: all who really seek to obey Jesus' teaching and accept Him as their Lord and Savior who paid the price for their sins.

Yes, it is My Unique Son Jesus who died for your sinfulness! But Who now lives! He has now sent and given you the Holy Spirit so that you may live righteously before Me.

Remember, this doesn't mean you will be perfect or always do the right thing. However, My children should always try to avoid doing bad or wrong things. This pleases Me and causes Me to be proud of you, My beloved.

You must also understand this extremely important saying or truth of Mine: If a person does not accept Jesus as My Son who died for their sins, they cannot be saved nor become My child (John 14:6).

Because I am a Holy God, and My people, Israel, were not holy or had a right heart towards Me, they were afraid. But I loved them and wanted to show them how to live in a way that was good and right.

So, I gave them My Law—the Ten Commandments or rules — to help them better understand My ways, which are always right. I wrote them on tablets of stone with My own finger.

Here are the **Ten Commandments** or rules I gave to Moses to give to My people:

1. "You shall have no other gods but Me." That means you must always put Me first in your life. These other gods are also evil spirit beings or people who reject Me.
2. "You shall not make any idols or images to worship." This means you cannot love anyone or any created thing more than Me.
3. "You shall not use My Name in a wrong way." You must always honor and revere My holy name.
4. "Remember the Sabbath Day and keep it holy." This now means that all My children are to honor Me everywhere and at all times.
5. "Honor your father and your mother." This means respecting and listening to your parents.
6. "Do not murder." Neither should you say harmful or hurtful things to others.
7. "Do not commit adultery." This means to be unfaithful to your husband or wife.
8. "Do not steal."
9. "Do not lie or say things that are not true about others."
10. "Do not covet or want what belongs to someone else." This means always being content and satisfied with what you have.

These rules show what is in My heart, even so, the love and honor you are to have for Me. And also the love and respect you are to express toward others.

My commandments are designed to help My children live in peace with others and understand what is good and acceptable behavior. Even so, the wrong behavior, which I disapprove of.

In addition, My Ten Commandments or laws show people that they need My help. This is because no mere mortal person can obey Me perfectly or do what is right and have pure thoughts all the time.

Let Me tell you why: it is because of the sinful nature that remains in everyone's corrupt bodies and thoughts. This also includes you, My child, and everyone who is born again.

That's why I said to My people, the children of Israel, that one day I would send someone greater than Moses. Someone who would obey Me completely! Someone who would speak on your behalf and bring you closer to Me.

My child, that someone is Jesus the Christ, My Immortal Son. He came into the world to make you righteous through His Self-sacrifice and to forgive you for your sinfulness.

The Bible says in Galatians 3:24, "The law was our schoolteacher to bring us to Christ." In other words, the law was given to teach My people how to live right and follow Me. As well as pointed to Jesus, who perfectly embodied My Laws.

Along with My Ten Commandments, there were also My very strict ceremonial laws that I commanded Israel to follow. These ceremonial laws and practices pointed to or foreshadowed the coming of My Son Jesus to Earth as the Lamb of God. He fulfilled My ceremonial laws through His Self-sacrifice.

Therefore, My ceremonial laws are no longer to be observed or performed... Now, Jesus is all you need!

When Moses climbed to the top of the mountain, he stayed with Me for forty days. He talked with Me and received My commands and ceremonial instructions.

However, below, the people grew impatient. They said, "Where is Moses? We don't know where he went!" So they told Aaron, Moses' brother, "Make us a god or an idol to follow!" This was not good! They should have waited for Moses so that he could speak on My behalf.

Aaron listened to them and made a golden calf out of their jewelry. The people danced around it! They sang and shouted for joy! But they broke My very first commandment! And so, I was very disappointed and became angry with My people!

When Moses came down from the mountain and saw them, he was also heartbroken and angry! He threw down the stone tablets, and they broke into many pieces. My anger was because My people had turned away from Me so quickly to follow after an idol, its god or wicked spirit.

How could they choose an image, a golden calf, that is associated with an evil spirit, which also means god, and its image to follow? And not Me, **The One True, Supreme God** who had delivered them from the bondage of Pharaoh.

I had just rescued them from Egypt, and now they were worshiping the statue or image of a false god, which is one with or associated with an evil spirit being or more! Do you remember that I told you that you and the angels are spirit persons, even as I, the LORD your God, is a Spirit?

(See John 4:24; Deuteronomy 4: 15,16).

It is critically important that you understand that I am the Supreme Spirit Person who created everything! I am the Almighty God! But all the angels, both the good ones and fallen angels, including yourself, who are human beings, are classified as gods, too.

I created both you and the angels, who are characterized as gods but without My Deity. I alone am the Almighty, Eternal One, Creator and God!

Mankind, this means you, My child and the heavenly angels who are created in My image do not possess My Divine nature. However, you were lovingly created to serve My purpose, mankind, here on earth, and My angels in heaven.

Now, back to Moses. Although He was angry with his people, as was I, he stood between the Israelites and Me. He, therefore, caused Me to stay or stop My wrath or judgment that I was ready to send upon My rebellious people!

He prayed for them and asked Me to forgive them. Moses was a good leader. He was a mediator—someone who stood in the middle to help others. This is what I also require of you, that you would pray for and help others.

However, even Moses could not make My people holy or righteous in My sight. Only Jesus, My Son and the **Great and Perfect Mediator,** can do that!

Jesus is, in fact, the Greater Mediator than Moses, the **Only One** who makes peace between Me and My children.

Jesus never sinned! He always listens to Me, and He gave His life to bring you back to Me and into Our family.

What You Should Learn and Remember:

1. God is holy, and His law shows us how to live.
2. The Ten Commandments teach us to love God and love others.
3. At times, all people are disobedient, and we need help.
4. Moses was a good leader, but Jesus is the perfect Mediator and our Helper.
5. God forgives us because He loves us.

Memory Verses:

A. "The law was our teacher to lead us to Christ." —Galatians 3:24
B. "I am the Lord your God... You shall have no other gods before Me." —Exodus 20:2-3
C. "Honor your father and your mother." —Exodus 20:12

Let's Talk:

1. Why did God give the Ten Commandments?
2. Why were the people afraid at the mountain?
3. What does it mean that Jesus is our Mediator?
4. How can we show love and obedience to God each day?

Prayer:

Dear God,

Thank You for Your Word and Your commandments.
Help me to love You with all my heart and to love others, too.
I know I can't be perfect, but I thank You for Jesus,
who obeyed You and helps me be close to You.
Thank You for teaching me right from wrong
and for loving me even when I make mistakes.
In Jesus' name, I pray. Amen.

CHAPTER 7

The Promised Land:
God Keeps His Promises

Hello, My sons and daughters! I hope you are doing well. Here's what I want you to learn in Chapter Seven.

I am the God who keeps My promises.
I am the God who leads and strengthens My people.
I give courage and victory to those who trust in Me.

Are you trusting Me? I hope you said yes!

(Scripture Reference: Joshua 1–6)

Do you remember how I led My people out of Egypt and through the wilderness? For forty years, they traveled, and I took care of them.

I gave them food from heaven and water from a rock. But the time came for them to go into the Promised Land—the land I promised to Abraham long ago.

But first, I needed to choose a new leader. My child Moses had grown very old and could no longer lead them. Besides, Moses had disobeyed

Me. Therefore, even though I loved him, he was not permitted to enter My promised land that I had given to the Israelites.

There was a brave man named Joshua.

He was one of the men who believed that, with My help, they could take the land, even when others were scared and did not trust or have faith in Me. Because of his faith and courage, I chose Joshua to lead My people after My child Moses died.

I spoke to Joshua and said, "Be strong and courageous! Do not be afraid. I will be with you wherever you go." (Joshua 1:9)

Joshua trusted Me. He knew that even though there were strong enemies in the land, like the Philistines, I was stronger! Joshua believed in My promise to give them the land.

Spies and Rahab's Faith

Joshua sent two spies into the city of Jericho to see what it was like.

There, they met a woman named Rahab. Rahab was not an Israelite, but she believed that I was the true God. She had heard how I parted the Red Sea and how I was with My people. She chose to help the spies because she wanted to be on My side.

Rahab hid them on her roof and kept them safe from the soldiers. When the spies thanked her, Rahab asked for one thing: she said, "Please save me and my family when your people take this city."

The spies promised, "Tie this red cord in your window, and we will make sure you and your family are safe." Rahab believed, and she did what they said.

I saved Rahab and her family because of her faith. Later, Rahab would become part of My big story, and she would be one of the great-great-grandmothers of Jesus!

Crossing the Jordan and the Battle of Jericho

Joshua led the people to the Jordan River. It was a big river, and they couldn't cross it on their own. But I showed them My power—again!

Just like at the Red Sea, I made the water stand up like a wall, and the people walked through on dry ground. They knew I was with them, just like I had been with Moses.

After crossing, they camped near Jericho, the strong, fortified walled city. The people in Jericho were scared because they had heard about how I helped and freed My people from Pharaoh. However, I had a unique plan for capturing and conquering this walled city!

I told Joshua, "Have the people march around the city once a day for six days. On the seventh day, march around it seven times. Then, the priests will blow their trumpets, and the people will shout. The walls will fall down!"

It didn't make sense to My people to win a battle that way, but Joshua obeyed Me. He did everything just as I said. When the people shouted, the walls of Jericho fell down flat! They went into the city and took it just as I promised.

Rahab and her family were saved because she trusted Me.

Joshua and the people praised Me for keeping My promise. I was with them, just as I said.

Joshua's Faith and God's Faithfulness

Joshua was a great leader because he trusted Me. He wasn't perfect, but he knew that I would keep My word. He was brave and strong because he knew I was by his side.

Rahab wasn't part of My people at first, but because of her faith, I brought her into My family. This shows that anyone who believes in Me can be part of My family!

What You Should Learn and Remember:

1. God always keeps His promises, no matter how hard things look.
2. Joshua was a strong leader because he trusted God.
3. Rahab's faith saved her, even when others didn't believe.
4. Sometimes, God's plans don't make sense to us, but obeying Him brings blessings.
5. God welcomes anyone who believes in Him, just like Rahab.

Memory Verses:

A. "Be strong and courageous. Do not be afraid; do not be discouraged, for the Lord your God will be with you wherever you go." —Joshua 1:9

B. "By faith, the walls of Jericho fell after the army had marched around them for seven days." —Hebrews 11:30

C. "By faith the prostitute Rahab, because she welcomed the spies, was not killed with those who were disobedient." —Hebrews 11:31

Let's Talk:

1. How did Joshua show his faith in God?
2. Why was Rahab saved when others in Jericho were not?
3. What does it mean to be strong and courageous in God?
4. How can you trust God when things seem hard or scary?

Prayer:

Dear God,

Thank You for always keeping Your promises.
Help me to be strong and courageous like Joshua,
and to trust You like Rahab did.
Even when things seem too hard,
I know You are with me.
Thank You for being a faithful and loving God.
In Jesus' name, I pray. Amen.

CHAPTER 8

The Judges: Everyone Did What Was Right in Their Own Eyes

Hello, My people. This is what I want you to know in Chapter Eight.

I am the God who calls My people to live holy lives.

I am the God who raises leaders when My people need help.

I am the God who sees your heart and can work through you, even when you make mistakes.

I am the God who always wins because My plans never fail.

I am the God who corrects My people because I love them.

I am the God who wants peace and good, not wars and fighting.

(Scripture References: Judges 1–21; Ruth 1–4; 1 Samuel 16-30; 2 Samuel 1-24; 1 Kings 1-11; 1 Chronicles 11-29; 2 Chronicles 1-9)

The Promised Land: A Special Place for God's People

Starting with the City of Jericho and then other pagan, ungodly or spiritually wicked Canaanite cities. I gave the Promised Land to My people. It was a very special land that I chose just for Israel.

This land was important because it was in a place where other nations could see them. I wanted My people, Israel, to live in this land in such a way that honored Me and to show others how good and holy I am.

Additionally, to let the other cities and nations know that I am the only True God and not the fallen gods or evil spirits they had chosen to follow.

My chosen people, also called the Hebrews or Jews, were supposed to be My light in the world—like a bright, shining example—to all the other nations.

It was My purpose for Israel that when the other cities and nations saw how they lived, followed My ways, and were blessed by Me – their God. These other people would come to know that I am the One True God and then choose to follow Me as well.

But something troubling happened!

Instead of being a light, My people, the Israelites, began to do what was wrong and embraced spiritual wickedness or darkness! They began to follow the wrong and wicked ways of the other nations–those belonging to this corrupt and evil world!

My people made idols after those of the pagan nations! They listened to these ungodly people and chose to follow after the evil ways of their gods–these rebellious and fallen spirit beings!

And so it was that My chosen people, the Israelites, rebelled and forgot about Me and did what was right in their own eyes. They were under the influence of their own sinful passions or desires. But, they had also come under the influence of wicked people and evil spirits.

This made Me sorrowful and full of righteous indignation. This means that there would be consequences for their wrongdoings or bad behavior resulting from not choosing to listen to or obey Me. I would have to punish or discipline My rebellious children, who I loved very much.

My beloved child, discipline can be called tough love. Its purpose is always to lovingly correct wrong behavior but also to lead you away from trouble and even harm or self-destruction (Hebrews 12: 6).

Now, My child, there's something important I must remind you to always think about: Behind all evil and the battles and struggles that My people face. There was something even bigger and more sinister going on; it is spiritual warfare!

Do you remember how, in My Garden of Eden, where Adam and Eve lived… then Satan, the evil spirit being, showed up to tempt Eve? Well, he came in an attempt to try to ruin My plan for My Kingdom to be established on Earth.

Even now, in this story, Satan, who is now working through the rebellious nations, didn't want Israel to live in the Promised Land. Satan understood that this land was part of My plan to bless the whole world and to establish My Kingdom on Earth.

Therefore, Satan tried to use the people already living in the land to fight against Israel and make them turn away from Me. But remember this, I always keep My promises!

No matter what Satan tries to do, My plans always come to pass! I always win, and so do My children when they keep their trust in Me.

When you and those who belong to Me obey Me, no matter what in this world is going on or what may happen to My beloved children... you and they are victorious with Me and because of My Son, Jesus!

Wars and Fighting: Why Do They Happen?

My children, I want you to know that I do not like wars. Wars happen because some people do bad things! People fight and hurt each other because they are sinners, and sin brings pain and trouble!

There were times, which was a long time ago, as you will see when you read the complete Bible stories, that I used Israel to correct the bad behavior of pagan nations when they did evil things.

Other times, again, a long time ago, I used other nations to also discipline Israel when My people disobeyed Me. Even though I hate war, I can still use it to teach lessons and help My people turn to Me in faith and to grow spiritually.

Remember, I always desire peace and goodness, not people fighting and hurting each other! I didn't send My Son, Jesus, to wage war on Earth, but rather to bring peace. And to reconcile or bring all people back to Me.

The Time of the Judges

After Joshua died, My chosen people no longer had a strong leader. Sometimes, they obeyed Me, but most of the time, they didn't. They disregarded and forgot My commandments and began worshiping or following false gods, just like their neighbors did.

They were following things or idols, just like the golden calf. The evil spirits caused people with sinful hearts or wrong thinking to listen to them and follow their evil ways. This is why they made idols. This was so disappointing to Me!

My people did not want to follow Me, their true and loving God. My people only wanted to do what they wanted to do! And not follow My perfect instructions that I had for them. This was not good. Their hearts were far from Me!

Because of their disobedience, they got into lots of trouble. I was so displeased with My children! But when they cried out for help, I showed My love and faithfulness towards them, and I gave judges to rescue My rebellious people.

Some judges were obedient or faithful teachers and leaders who helped My people when they were in trouble. While others were corrupt and rebellious towards Me. These judges misled Israel, who corrupted themselves and dishonored Me.

When my people rejected My ways, they became weak and vulnerable. This was when Satan tried to use their enemies to destroy My people. It was then that I gave these judges to protect and lead My people back to Me! However, unfortunately, not all the judges were good leaders.

Some of them did not listen to Me and led Israel astray. When that happened, the people made even worse choices and got into even greater trouble! When My people are disobedient, there are often consequences, and sometimes those consequences can be very bad!

Oftentimes, I allow those consequences because I want My people to learn from their mistakes. Even when I personally correct or discipline My people, I never stop loving them!

I may feel disappointed, but My love for them never ends. When you make mistakes or do wrong, I will always love you, too! However, you should learn and grow rather than continue to make poor choices... Okay?

Deborah – A Wise and Brave Leader

One of the judges was a woman named Deborah. She was very wise and loved Me with all her heart!

When my people, Israel, were in trouble because of their enemies, Deborah trusted Me. She encouraged a man named Barak to lead the army, but Barak was afraid to go without her.

Deborah agreed to go along and helped lead the people to victory because she was brave and full of faith! Deborah demonstrated that being a leader means trusting in Me, her God and helping others find the courage to be brave, too.

Now, my children, I want you to know that this was not My plan.

Just as I did not plan for wars, which are often caused by bad or sinful people, I did not plan for Deborah, this courageous and wise woman, to lead the battle.

I wanted the men to take on this responsibility to be good leaders in their families and My family, now called the Church. What church or place of worship do you attend? Are there good leaders there? I hope that you are a good and faithful leader as well.

Once again, because Barak was afraid, I permitted Deborah to help Israel. Sometimes, I use people in unique situations who might not usually lead because I want to accomplish My purpose. This was the case with Deborah in this unique situation and desperate times for Israel.

This teaches us that I can use anyone, but you must always remember to trust and obey My ways, as well as the leadership order and structure that I have planned for your home and My Church.

(See: Ephesians 5:22,23; 1 Corinthians 11:3; Colossians 3:18–21; 1 Peter 3: 1–7; 1 Timothy 3:1– 13; Titus 1: 5-9).

Gideon – The Man Who Was Afraid

Another judge was named Gideon.

When I chose Gideon, he was hiding from his enemies because he was so scared! I sent a good angel as a messenger to tell him, "The Lord is with you, mighty warrior!" Gideon didn't feel like a mighty warrior, but I saw what he could become.

I also see what you can become if you choose to follow and listen to Me. Even though Gideon was unsure, he obeyed Me. With just 300 men, Gideon defeated Satan's huge enemy army of people because Gideon learned to put his trust in Me.

This army of lost and rebellious people that Gideon fought against were following Satan's plan and, therefore, would not listen to Me. However, they were also following their evil hearts, which was mainly their problem.

Because of their stubborn hearts, there would be consequences for their actions… I sent Gideon and his army! Gideon learned that when you trust Me, your God, even when you may feel small and afraid, I can do great things through people who put their hope and faith in Me.

Samson – The Strong Man Who Made Mistakes

There was also a judge named Samson; he was very strong! His physical strength came from a special promise because of Samson's Nazarite vow he made to Me. He was never to cut his hair, drink alcohol or touch anything considered by My Law at the time to be unclean.

But Samson had a problem—he didn't always make good choices. He was proud of his strength or personal ability and didn't always listen to Me. Even though Samson made many mistakes, I still loved him and forgave him when he asked.

Samson learned that being strong on the inside—by trusting Me—is more important than being strong on the outside or self-reliant. When Samson did listen to Me, I helped him win battles over the ungodly Philistine people who did not obey Me.

Ruth – The Loyal and Faithful Woman

During the time of the judges, there was a woman named Ruth. Ruth wasn't from Israel, but she loved her mother-in-law, Naomi, and loved Me.

Naomi was from the tribe of Israel. She loved and honored Me; she was a bright, shining light, a good example, as she showed her trust in Me. This was why Ruth learned to love Me: Naomi honored Me and, thereby, set a great example for Ruth to follow.

Are you setting a good example for others? Are you following the good example of others, such as your parents and other godly people, who trust and love Me?

Ruth shows that I see the faithfulness of your heart, and I bless those who choose to follow Me. Because of this, Ruth would become the great-grandmother of King David, the family lineage that Jesus would come through.

King David and His Son, King Solomon

After the time of the Judges, I raised up a shepherd boy named David to be the king of Israel. David was a man after My own heart. He honored Me and was known for his faith and courage. As a young man, he defeated the evil giant Goliath with just a sling and a stone.

Goliath and his army had fought against My people, Israel. He and his people were being used by wicked spiritual forces, Satan's army, to oppose My children and Me, their Creator. I chose David because of his faithfulness, and he became one of Israel's greatest kings.

He made Jerusalem the capital and brought the Ark of the Covenant there, uniting the people in worship of Me. Though David made some great mistakes, he always sought My forgiveness.

I, therefore, made a promise to David that in the distant future, his descendant would be the Messiah and his Great King, who would sit on My throne and rule forever!

This descendant of King David would become and now is My Unique— One of a Kind Son, Jesus, the King of kings!

David's son, Solomon, became king after him. Solomon was known for his wisdom, a gift from Me, and he built the great temple in Jerusalem— a beautiful place where My people came to worship Me, the One True God.

Solomon's wisdom, which he asked Me for, and achievements made Israel a powerful and prosperous nation! Sadly, Solomon's heart turned away from Me later in his life. This was because he did not follow My commandments fully.

Resulting from Solomon's disobedience, his actions led to Israel's division as a nation after his death. Israel became Northern Israel, and in the southern territory that I had given to My people, they were known as the Kingdom of Judah.

From the name Judah, My people began to embrace the identity or name 'Jew' or, collectively, the Jewish Nation.

What You Should Learn and Remember:

1. God doesn't like wars, but they often occur because of the sinful actions of people.
2. God uses people who make mistakes, and if we trust Him, He can still work through us.
3. Even when we make mistakes, God never stops loving us.
4. God wants men to lead in certain roles, but sometimes He uses women, such as Deborah, when the need arises.
5. God always wins and keeps His promises, even when things look hard.
6. God values a heart for Him: David's sincere love for God teaches us the importance of having a heart that seeks after God.
7. Wisdom comes from God: Solomon's wisdom reminds us to ask God for guidance in making good choices.
8. God can use imperfect people: David and Solomon's lives show that God can still use us despite our mistakes.
9. The importance of finishing well: Solomon's later struggles teach us to stay faithful to God throughout our lives.
10. God's promises stand: God kept His promise to David, reminding us that His word is always true.

Memory Verse:

A. "In those days, there was no king in Israel. Everyone did what was right in his own eyes." — Judges 21:25

Let's Talk:

1. Why did Israel keep turning away from God?

2. What did the judges do for the people?
3. How was Ruth's story different from the rest?
4. What made David a good leader, even with his mistakes?
5. Why did Solomon ask God for wisdom?
6. How can we learn from both their strengths and weaknesses?

Prayer:

Dear Father,

Thank You for loving me even when I make mistakes.
Help me learn to do what is right and trust You.
Teach me to be brave like Deborah, faithful like Ruth, and strong on the inside like Samson.
Thank You for guiding me even when I don't understand.
In Jesus' name, I pray. Amen.

CHAPTER 9

Wisdom and Worship: Lessons from the Books of Job, Psalms, Proverbs, Ecclesiastes, and Song of Solomon

Hello, My child, I hope you are doing well. Here's what I want you to learn in Chapter Nine.

I am the God who gives wisdom and understanding.
I am the God who is with you when life is hard.
I am the God who deserves worship and praise.
I am the God who teaches you how to live well.
I am the God who loves you and makes love beautiful.

Job – Trusting God When Life Is Hard

Sometimes, bad things happen to good people.

In the Bible, there was a man named Job who reverenced or honored Me! Job was kind, honest, and faithful to Me, his God. He had a large family and a number of animals. Job was blessed by Me, spiritually and materially.

One day, Satan, this fallen angel who was once called Lucifer, came to Me. He said that Job only loved Me because his life was easy because of My favor or blessing on Job's life. So, I allowed Satan to test Job to see if he would still love Me even when things got hard.

I Allowed Bad Things at the Hands of Satan to Happen to Job

Suddenly, Job lost everything—his animals, his home, and even his children. Job became very sick and felt alone. Even his friends thought he must have done something bad to deserve such trouble.

But Job knew he had done nothing wrong. He felt confused and sad, but he didn't stop talking to Me. Job, this righteous man didn't understand why he was suffering, but he still trusted Me.

Why Do Bad Things Happen?

It's essential to recognize that not all bad things occur because of Satan or due to someone's wrongdoing. Sometimes, bad things happen because You live in a broken world where there is destruction, sickness, pain, sadness and death.

One day, I will stop all bad things from happening! But for now, I want you to always trust Me, just like Job did.

Job's story was a special situation that I permitted to show you that even when life is hard, you can still trust Me, your God. Because Job never stopped believing or trusting in Me, everything he lost, I restored or gave back to him.

Although you and My faithful children may face many difficulties and feel lost in this world, as did Job. Nevertheless, if you keep your faith in Me, like Job, know that when I create the New Heaven and Earth, I am going to give back to you everybody that you lost to death and more!

I will restore the glory of My people and make all things new, just as I did for Job. Until that day of My restoration, always keep your trust in Me, no matter how bad things get.

What Can We Learn from Job?

1. Trust God even when you don't understand.
2. Talk to God about your feelings—He listens.
3. Know that God is always good, even when life is not.
4. One day, God will make everything right and new.

Psalms – Songs and Prayers from the Heart

Have you ever sung a song when you were happy? Or prayed to Me when you felt sad or scared? The Book of Psalms is full of songs, prayers, poems and praise that people wrote to Me, their God.

King David wrote many of these psalms. You can see from his writing that he was sometimes happy and, at other times, afraid. No matter what, David always talked to Me about his feelings.

Why Should We Read the Psalms?

1. They teach us how to worship and praise God.
2. They show us how to pray when we feel happy, sad, or scared.

3. They remind us that God is with us no matter what.

Memory Verse:

"The Lord is my shepherd; I shall not want." — Psalm 23:1

Proverbs – Wise Words for Life

Have you ever heard someone say, "Think before you act?"

The Book of Proverbs is full of wise sayings to help you make good choices. King Solomon, known as the wisest man, wrote many of these proverbs. He wanted to teach people how to live in a way that pleases Me.

Why Should We Read Proverbs?

1. They teach us to be wise and kind.
2. They help us make good decisions.
3. They remind us to respect God in everything we do.

Memory Verse:

"The fear of the Lord is the beginning of wisdom." — Proverbs 9:10

Ecclesiastes – What Really Matters

Have you ever wondered, "What's the point of life?"

The Book of Ecclesiastes asks big questions about why you live and what really matters.

King Solomon wrote this book to convey and emphasize that life without Me, your God, is meaningless and empty. Even if you have money, toys, or lots of friends, your life is not truly happy and complete without Me.

Solomon teaches us that the best way to live is to love and obey Me.

Why Should We Read Ecclesiastes?

1. It teaches us to focus on what really matters—God.
2. It helps us understand that stuff doesn't make us happy—God does.
3. It reminds us that life is a gift from God, and we should honor Him.

Memory Verse:

"Fear God and keep His commandments, for this is the whole duty of man." — Ecclesiastes 12:13

Song of Solomon – A Song About Love

I made love to be a wonderful and beautiful thing!

The Song of Solomon is a unique book that illustrates the ideal relationship between a husband and wife. It reminds you that I made marriage to be a happy, loving, caring, and intimate relationship.

Just as I gave Eve to Adam as his wife, My plan is for a man and a woman to come together under My guidance in marriage. When a man and a woman get married, if they choose, they may have children and become a loving family!

This is My perfect plan for a man and a woman: to love each other, to have children, and to follow Me together as a family, even so, as My spiritual family. This kind of love expressed through family is special and beautiful because it reflects My glory and love for you.

Why Should We Read Song of Solomon?

1. It shows that sexual intimacy and love is a gift from God.
2. It teaches us that marriage is part of God's good plan.
3. It reminds us of God's great love for His people.

What Can We Learn?

1. Bad things happen, but God is always with us.
2. Worship and praise God, just like in the Psalms.
3. Seek wisdom through God's words, just like in Proverbs.
4. Focus on God because He gives life meaning, as Ecclesiastes teaches.
5. Love deeply and purely, as shown in the Song of Solomon.
6. Even when life is confusing or disheartening, trust God because He cares for you.

Memory Verse:

"Trust in the Lord with all your heart." — Proverbs 3:5

Let's Talk:

1. What can we learn from Job's suffering?
2. How do the Psalms help us worship God?
3. What kind of wisdom is found in Proverbs?
4. Why does Ecclesiastes say life without God is empty?
5. What does the Song of Solomon teach about love and devotion?
6. How can we apply wisdom to our lives today?

Prayer:

Dear God,

Thank You for teaching me to trust You, even when life is hard.
Help me to praise You like David did and to make wise choices like Solomon.
Thank You for loving me and for showing me what true love looks like.
Help me to love others with kindness.
In Jesus' name, Amen.

CHAPTER 10

The Exile: Sin Has Its Consequences

Hello, I'm so happy that you enjoy learning about Me from the Bible and this book. Here is what I want you to know in Chapter Ten.

I am the God who calls you to follow Me.
I am the God who warns you when you go the wrong way.
I am the God who stays with you, even when you face hard times.
I am the God who wants you to be faithful to Me.
I am the God who rewards faithfulness.

Consequences of Sin – Israel's Disobedience

(Scripture References: 2 Kings 17, 25; Daniel 1; Ezekiel 1-3, 18)

Do you remember the judges and kings of Israel? Some of them were good leaders, but many were bad leaders who disobeyed Me. When the bad judges ruled, they led the people–Israel away from Me.

My people started worshiping idols and doing horrible things that caused Me grief. I sent My anointed and chosen prophets to warn them, but they didn't listen to them. I told Israel through My prophets that there would be great consequences for their disobedience.

I Use Other Nations for Discipline

When you read your Bible, you will see in the Old Testament, specifically and exclusively, how and why I sometimes use other nations to correct Israel?

Well, this is what happened. The Northern Kingdom of Israel: they were especially rebellious and corrupt or evil! They had many wicked kings who led My people away from Me.

So, I used the Assyrian nation, a powerful and feared people, to conquer the Northern Kingdom of Israel. The Assyrians captured My people and took them away from their homes.

This was My way of correcting or punishing Israel for their sin and idolatry against Me. Later, the Southern Kingdom of Judah also disobeyed Me. Accordingly, I allowed another powerful nation, Babylon, to conquer Judah.

The Babylonians captured My people and took them to Babylon. This time was called the Exile because My people were forced to leave the Promised Land. It was a sad time, but I never stopped loving them. Even when they were far from home, I stayed with them.

Faithful Boys in a Strange Land: Daniel, Shadrach, Meshach, and Abednego

When the enemy kings took over, they captured young boys from Israel. Among those boys were Daniel, Shadrach, Meshach, and Abednego. They were taken far from their home to Babylon, where these people did not worship Me.

Even though they were far away, Israel knew that they were still My chosen people. They yearned greatly to return home. One day in the future, at My appointed time, I was going to return them to their promised land.

Staying Faithful to Me

The king of Babylon wanted them to eat special food that I said not to eat. But Daniel and his friends asked for different food because they wanted to obey Me. I blessed them for being faithful, and they grew strong and wise.

Standing Up for Me: The Fiery Furnace

One day, the Babylonian king created a large golden statue and instructed everyone to bow down and worship it. Shadrach, Meshach, and Abednego knew that worshiping idols was wrong.

They said, "We will not bow down. We only worship God!"

The king got very angry and threw them into a fiery furnace! But guess what? I protected them! The king looked inside the furnace and saw not just three but four people! I was with them in the fire!

When they came out, not even a hair on their heads was burned! The king was amazed and praised Me.

I Reveal the Future: Another Grand Statue and My Kingdom

One night, the king of Babylon had a strange dream that he did not understand. He saw a huge statue made with a head of gold, arms and chest of silver, a belly of bronze, legs of iron, and feet of clay and iron.

Then, a stone that was not cut or made by human hands came from heaven and destroyed the statue! I helped Daniel understand the dream. Daniel said to the king: the statue you dreamt about represented powerful nations that would rule on Earth.

The stone was My Son Jesus, which would break all other kingdoms and last forever! One day, My Son Jesus will return, and My Kingdom will rule the world! Even when nations rise and fall, My Son's Kingdom will be the greatest of all and will remain for all eternity!

My Prophet Ezekiel

During this sad and difficult time of Israel's exile, I also spoke through Ezekiel to remind My people to repent and turn back to Me. Ezekiel warned them that their sin had consequences. And this was why Israel had been taken captive.

But he also shared hope that I would bring them back to their land someday.

I never forget My promises, and I will always love My people!

What You Should Learn and Remember:

1. Disobedience has consequences. I don't ignore sin, but I discipline because I love you.
2. Even when you make mistakes, I won't leave you. I still care for you.
3. You can be faithful to Me even when others aren't.
4. I can protect you when you are in trouble.
5. Sometimes, I allow difficult situations to teach you to trust Me more.
6. One day, Jesus will return, and My Kingdom will rule forever.
7. I don't want you to learn the hard way by making mistakes repeatedly.
8. I want you to learn what to do by reading the Bible and listening to your parents.
9. If you listen to Me and those I place over you, you can avoid many mistakes and consequences.

Memory Verse:

"Be strong and courageous. Do not be afraid or terrified because of them, for the Lord your God goes with you; He will never leave you nor forsake you." — Deuteronomy 31:6

Let's Talk:

1. Why were God's people taken into exile?
2. What sins led to their punishment?
3. How did the people feel in a foreign land?
4. What did the prophets say during the exile?

5. How did God show mercy during this time?

6. What can we learn about obeying God today?

Prayer:

Dear God,

Thank You for being with me, even when I am in hard places.
Help me to be like Daniel and his friends, who stayed faithful to You no matter what.
Teach me to trust You when things don't go my way.
Help me to listen to You and to those who love me so I don't have to learn the hard way.
Thank You for protecting me and keeping me safe. In Jesus' name, Amen.

CHAPTER 11

The Return: Coming Back Home and Rebuilding

Hello, My dear children. I want to tell you about how I brought My people–Israel, back home from captivity after their long, difficult time in a foreign land.

I am the God who keeps His promises.
I am the God who forgives when My people repent.
I am the God who restores and rebuilds.
I am the God who guides and helps faithful leaders.
I am the God who teaches you to pray and to trust Me.

Coming Back Home

(Scripture References: Ezra; Nehemiah; Haggai 1-2)

Do you remember how My people were taken away as captives from their homes because of their disobedience towards Me? They had been in exile for many years. But they remained My chosen people Who I loved, and some of them remembered this.

Even though they were far away, I promised that one day, I would bring them back to the land that I had given to My people, Israel. And just as I promised, I did!

After many years, I moved the heart of a new king to let My people return home. They went back to Jerusalem, their special city.

But when they arrived, they found their homes and the temple in ruins. Everything needed to be rebuilt. Even though the temple and the city were being rebuilt, the temple merely served as a mirror or foreshadowing of something much greater to come!

One day, Jesus will build a new home and Kingdom for all My children! It will be a perfect place where there is no more sadness, no more trouble, no more evil, and no more death!

You will live together with Me, forever, in a New Heaven and Earth! This new home will be a place of joy and peace!

My Son Jesus, the King of kings, will stand before His people as the **Living Temple**! All of My children are also called **living temples**. This means that you are one with Jesus and Me! And just like My Son Jesus, you are to love and serve Me (John 2:19-22; Matthew 12:6; 1 Corinthians 3:16).

Why the Temple Is Important

My children, do you know why the temple was so important to My people? The temple was the special place where I met with them. While there, they worshipped Me, and their sacrifices or gifts were offered to Me, their God. Their actions showed their love and obedience towards Me.

The temple reminded them that I was with them. When the temple was destroyed, it felt like a part of their connection with Me was broken. But I wanted to restore that connection, so I helped them rebuild the temple.

The temple being rebuilt was like a new beginning for My people, reminding them that I still loved them and wanted to be close to them. However, one day, Jesus would come, and He has come to show that He Himself was the perfect way to know Me and worship Me!

But for Israel, rebuilding the temple helped My people feel close to Me again. Today, I call My children living temples because the Holy Spirit dwells within you; therefore, you belong to Me, your Living God!

This means that you have become sanctified or that you have been separated from the world to represent Me as a bright, shining light on Earth. Like Jesus, you are My living temples who are to share your love and serve Me and others.

My children, you must always listen to Me and follow My instructions. This is why you should obey Me: just like Israel's temple was destroyed, and they also faced opposition for their disobedience. Even still, opposition came from their enemies when it was time to rebuild.

Listen, if you are not obedient to Me. Satan also greatly desires to tear you down or destroy you, My living temples. If you allow him to do so through your rebellion against Me, your God.

Satan eagerly wants to keep you from growing strong in Me as My living temple and shining light in this evil and dark world.

Faithful Leaders for a Big Job

Zerubbabel: Rebuilding the Temple

One of the faithful leaders I used was Zerubbabel. He led Israel in initiating the rebuilding of the temple. This was a big job because the temple was torn down and destroyed. But Zerubbabel trusted Me and encouraged the people to work together.

I sent My prophets Haggai and Zechariah to encourage him and the others. They reminded the people that I was with them!

Ezra: Bringing Back Worship

After the temple was built, I sent Ezra, one of My faithful leaders. Ezra loved My Word and wanted to teach it to the people. He led them to worship Me the right way again. Ezra reminded them of how important it is to obey My Word.

He prayed for the people and taught them to pray as well. I love it when My children pray to Me because it shows they trust Me! Are you learning to put your trust in Me?

Nehemiah: Rebuilding the Walls

Another leader I sent was Nehemiah. He heard that Jerusalem's walls were still broken down, and that made him sad. Nehemiah prayed and asked Me for help.

I gave him the courage to talk to the king, and the king let him go to rebuild the walls. Nehemiah faced many troubles and enemies, but he didn't give up. He kept praying and working hard!

With My help, the people rebuilt the walls in just 52 days! Nehemiah's faith and perseverance were a big example to the people.

Looking Ahead to My Greatest Prophet

Do you remember that long ago, I used Moses as one of My great prophets? He spoke for Me and led My people out of Egypt.

But I had promised My people that one day, I would send My Greatest Prophet of all—Jesus, My unique Son! My Son Jesus actually came to Earth to visit with My chosen people, Israel and all My people everywhere, just over 2,000 years ago.

Unlike any other prophet, My Son Jesus would be the Perfect and sinless Leader. He would unite all people with Him; this My Greatest Prophet, the King of kings and Israel's long-awaited Messiah!

Jesus would and has spoken My truth and shown My love like no one else! Even so, the prophets during Ezra and Nehemiah's time looked forward to Jesus' coming. He would and has brought true renewal and saved My children from this present evil world of sin!

Here is something else I want you to know: Jesus, under the power of the Holy Spirit, inspired select men to write the Bible for you and everyone in the whole world. He wants you to learn about Us, the Holy and Divine Trinity–Me, God the Father, Jesus My Son and the Holy Spirit!

Together, we all become one big happy family! How you become My sons and daughters, My family on Earth, is provided in the New Testament of the Bible. The Old Testament of the Bible foretold or pointed to this taking place.

In the New Testament, it shows, and you learn how My prophecies and promises are perfectly fulfilled in and through Jesus!

A Big Transition: The New Testament or New Covenant

My children, this is the final chapter to be discussed of the Old Testament, also known as the Old Covenant. Under My Old Testament, I uniquely dealt with My people, Israel, through ceremonial laws that pointed to the life of Jesus and fulfilled in the ministry of My Son.

Do you remember some of the things that you have already learned about Jesus?... Yes, He would be My promised Messiah and King, the Lamb of God, who is to come into this corrupt world to cleanse all people of their sins.

Yes, it was Jesus who prophesied or who was spoken about in Genesis 3:15 and many other places throughout the Old Testament.

Here's something that I did not discuss with you earlier. My Son, Jesus, sometimes appeared in the Old Testament as a Mighty Spirit Being—the **Angel of the Lord** (Genesis 16:7-13; Genesis 22:11-18; Exodus 3:2-6; Judges 2:1-4 and elsewhere).

However, it is in the New Testament that something amazing will happen! Jesus will come and be born on Earth, just like you were born. The Son of God will actually clothe Himself in flesh. Do you remember when I talked to you about you putting on your clothing?

Well, Jesus, who is a Spirit Person, is going to put on or cover Himself with a perfect body that is free from sin and the desire and inclination to do bad things.

Jesus is My very Unique Son. He does not have an earthly father who helped Him come into existence. What makes Him Unique is that He and I are **One**. This means that Jesus, like Me, His Father, in essence or in every way, is God and is one with Me and the Holy Spirit.

Jesus has always existed, meaning He was not created. This is one of Our amazing mysteries! It is by faith that you are to accept this; Our truth, the Holy Trinity, as presented or seen throughout the Bible.

In the New Testament, you will see that Jesus was born bodily by the Power of the Holy Spirit and gifted to His earthly mother, Mary. Jesus will be shown walking on Earth as the True Light of the world, who frees and leads His followers away from sinful lifestyle choices.

You will learn more about His life of service, His love, and His great sacrifice as the Lamb of God who died for your sins and the sinful practices of all people. And because He was perfect in all of His ways, Jesus, by the Power of the Holy Spirit, overcame the grave and defeated death!

Because Jesus now lives forever, those who turn away from following their sinful ways and who will instead follow Him will also live forever with Jesus in My Kingdom!

I can't wait to tell you more about Him! And for that great day that you and all of My children will live with Me forever!

What You Should Learn and Remember:

1. Faithful leaders make a difference by trusting Me and helping others.
2. Even when things seem broken, I can rebuild and restore.
3. Praying is important when you face big challenges.
4. Perseverance means not giving up, even when it's hard.
5. I can use anyone who is willing to obey Me.
6. Under the Old Covenant, the temple was a special place for My people to meet with Me.
7. I always send the right people to help My people return to Me.
8. I planned from the beginning to send My Greatest Prophet, Messiah, King and very Son, Jesus, to rescue you from sin and death and to guide you.
9. Now that Jesus has become the Living Temple, My earthly sons and daughters are also living temples.

Memory Verse:

"Be strong and courageous. Do not be afraid; do not be discouraged, for the Lord your God will be with you wherever you go." — Joshua 1:9

Let's Talk:

1. Why were God's people sent into exile?
2. What did it mean for them to come back home?
3. How did they rebuild the temple and the walls?
4. What challenges did they face while rebuilding?
5. Why is it important to obey God's Word?
6. How does God help us start over when we fail?

Prayer:

Dear LORD,

Thank You for always being with us, even when we feel far away.
Help us to trust You, just like Zerubbabel, Ezra, and Nehemiah did.
Teach us to pray, work hard, and never give up when we face hard times.
Thank You for sending Jesus, the greatest leader and prophet, to show us
Your love.
Help us to follow Him every day.
In Jesus' name, Amen.

CHAPTER 12

The Birth of Jesus:
God Becomes Man

Hello, family. I want to share with you the most wonderful part of My miraculous story! This is when I came to be with you through My Son, Jesus, who is My exact image (Hebrews 1:3; Colossians 1:15; John 14:9).

This is what I want you to learn from this chapter:

I am the God who keeps My promises.
I am the God who brings Light into darkness.
I am the God who fulfills prophecy.
I am the God who came as a man to save the world.
I am the God for whom nothing is too hard.

A Very Special Announcement

(Scripture References: Luke 1-2; Matthew 1:18-25; Isaiah 7:14; Micah 5:2; Genesis 3:15)

Long ago, I promised that one day, I would send My Special Savior and Redeemer to rescue My people from sin and death. Even after Adam and

Eve sinned in the Garden of Eden, I promised that one day, the "Seed of the woman would crush the serpent's head!"

This prophecy pointed to My Son, Jesus, who would defeat Satan, all sickness and evil and bring Salvation to the world! Now, as presented in the New Testament of the Bible, it was time for that promise to come true!

Just as I spoke, My Word at the beginning of time, as you understand time. And Heaven and Earth came into being. I also decreed by My Word, and Jesus, by the Power of the Holy Spirit, came to the world through His earthly mother, Mary, born bodily or clothed Himself in flesh.

My Son Jesus, Who is One with Me, was and is God, who also chose to become as man or human, but without a sinful nature (John 1:1-5). I did this for you, My child! I came to deliver you from the evil of sin, just as I delivered the Israelites from the evil of Pharaoh.

There is nothing too hard for Me!... I am God... I am Almighty!

I did not need a man, like you needed your earthly father, to help Me bring Jesus, My eternally existing Son, into the world. You see, I sent the Holy Spirit to overshadow Mary, and My Son was formed or took bodily shape in her womb; this is called the Virgin Birth.

The Holy Spirit has been working since the beginning of time, just like when He moved over the waters at creation to fashion Heaven and Earth. Jesus' virgin birth was both unique and supernatural! He was, in fact, conceived and fashioned bodily by the Holy Spirit!

This had always been My plan. However, as I've stated before, I created the angels, you and everyone with free will to make choices. I knew that some of My angels and people would not obey or listen to Me. Therefore, you would need Jesus as your Redeemer because of rebellion.

There is even more that I will teach you about God—the Holy Spirit, shortly. But for now, as I have also previously shared with you, I am God, Three-in-One; God the Father, God the Son, and God the Holy Spirit. Together, We form or make up what many call the Holy Trinity.

Mary: A Humble Heart

I chose a young woman named Mary to be the mother of My Son. She was a virgin. This means that Mary had not been sexually intimate with Joseph or anyone.

Mary lived in a town called Nazareth, and she was kind, humble, and full of faith. One day, I sent the angel Gabriel to speak to her. Gabriel said, "Greetings, favored one! The Lord is with you."

Mary was surprised and a little afraid, but Gabriel said, "Do not be afraid, Mary, for you have found favor with God. You will have a son, and you shall call His name Jesus."

Gabriel explained that Jesus would be great and would be called the Son of the Most High God! Mary wondered how this could happen since she wasn't married yet. Gabriel told her, "The Holy Spirit will come upon you, and the Power of the Most High God will overshadow you."

Even though it was unexpected and quite a surprise for Mary, nonetheless, she trusted Me and said, "I am the Lord's servant. Let it be done to me according to your word."

Mary's faith and obedience made Me extremely proud of her! Mary's faith demonstrates the faith and trust that I want all people to have in Me. With this, I am well pleased!

Joseph: A Kind and Righteous Man

Mary was engaged to Joseph, but they had not gotten married to become a husband and wife. When Joseph found out that Mary was going to have a baby, he was confused and troubled because they had not become a husband and wife.

They had not shared in My gift, given to a married couple—a man and woman. That is, My special gift to this union under My design, called sexual intimacy, which is expressed and shared between a husband and his wife.

Husbands and their wives are part of My very good and perfect plan! Yes, I planned from the very beginning, just as with Adam and Eve, for a man and a woman to love each other, get married, and become husband and wife, and even dads and moms.

My plan, and it remains the same today, is for husbands and their wives, a man and a woman, to have wonderful and smart children who would obey and love Me just as their parents do. My plan was for this earthly family to also become one with Me as My spiritual family on Earth.

And so, on one special night, I sent an angel to Joseph in a dream to share My wonderful plan with him.

The angel said, "Joseph, do not be afraid to take Mary as your wife, for the child conceived in her is from the Holy Spirit. You shall call His name Jesus, for He will save His people from their sins."

Joseph believed and trusted Me. He, therefore, took Mary as his wife and cared for her and baby Jesus after He was born. Yes, both Mary and her husband took great care of My Unique Son, Jesus, when He was a baby and as He grew into an adult.

Joseph's faithfulness showed that he was a good and righteous man. I was so proud of Joseph and Mary because they had faith in Me, their God.

The Birth of My Unique Son Jesus

One day, Caesar Augustus, the ruler, said that everyone must go to their hometown to be counted. This was called a census.

Mary and Joseph traveled to Bethlehem, their home. But when they got there, there was no room in the inn for them to stay. So, they stayed in a stable where the animals were kept. There, My Unique Son, Jesus, was born and gifted to Mary.

Mary wrapped Him in swaddling clothes and laid Him in a manger. It wasn't a fancy or nice place, but it was part of My plan to show that Jesus came into the world humbly. I was going to take care of them even as I am now taking care of you.

They would experience challenging and difficult times, just as you and everyone else do. But they always believed and trusted in Me, their God and Father.

Are you trusting in Me? I know that you are, even though life can be tough at times.

The Angels and the Shepherds

On a special night that I appointed, there were shepherds in the fields watching over their sheep.

These shepherds were not just humble men, but they were also considered wise because they were faithful and diligent as they waited for My promise of their Deliverer. They knew that My Son and their Messiah and King would soon be born!

Suddenly, an angel whom I had sent appeared and said to them, "Do not be afraid! I bring you Good News of great joy. Today in the city of David, a Savior has been born to you; He is Christ the Lord."

Then, many of My good and obedient angels appeared, singing, "Glory to God in the highest!" The angels were full of joy because they knew that I sent My Son, Jesus, to save the world! Yes, baby Jesus was God! This was why the angels praised Him, and the wise men gave Jesus gifts.

I have many angels who serve Me and help My people. Most of the time, they are invisible, but every now and then, I allow them to be seen.

But remember, just as I have good angels, there are fallen angels—bad angels who work for Satan. These evil angels do bad things and deceive or mislead My people into doing bad things.

They lead people to do bad things through the horrible actions or words that are seen and heard on television, through the computer or personal devices you have and even through some misleading songs and music!

This is why I sent Jesus: He came to fight against evil and to save you from sin!

This is why you must read your Bible: so that you can also learn to recognize all kinds of evil and, spiritually, through prayer and watchfulness, resist or fight against evil so that you do not do evil things.

And so, after hearing the message from the angel, the shepherds hurried to find baby Jesus. When they saw Him, they worshiped Him and rejoiced!

They were the first to hear that the Savior of the world, My Son Jesus, had come to Earth to deliver His people from sin, from evil and the fear of death!

What You Should Learn and Remember:

1. God keeps His promises, even when it takes a long time.
2. Humility and faith bring joy to my heart.
3. Jesus is the light of the world, born to bring Salvation.
4. I chose ordinary people to be part of My great plan.
5. You don't have to be rich or important for Me to love you and use you.
6. Angels serve Me and help My people, but there are also evil angels who work for Satan.
7. Nothing is too hard for Me—I can do miracles and work in unexpected ways.

Memory Verse:

"For unto you is born this day in the city of David a Savior, who is Christ the Lord." — Luke 2:11

Let's Talk:

1. Who were Jesus' earthly parents?
2. Why was Jesus born in a stable?
3. What did the angels say about Jesus?
4. Why did the shepherds visit Jesus?
5. What made Jesus' birth so special?
6. How can we celebrate Jesus' birth today?

Prayer:

Dear God,

Thank You for sending Your Son, Jesus, to be the Light of the world. Help us to have faith like Mary, obedience like Joseph, and joy like the shepherds.

Thank You for keeping Your promises and loving us so much.

I want to follow You with a humble heart.

In Jesus' name, Amen.

CHAPTER 13

The Ministry of Jesus: The Kingdom Has Come

Hello, My family of believers. I want to tell you about the most amazing time when My Son, Jesus, began His ministry on Earth. When Jesus started His work on Earth, it was a sign that My Spiritual Kingdom had come on Earth!

Jesus came to reveal My heart, to heal the broken, to teach the truth, and to defeat the evil powers of darkness! He came to show everyone who **I am** and how much I love them. He taught people how to live righteously and gave hope to those who were lost and hurting.

The Early Years of Jesus

(Scripture Reference: Luke 2:41-52)

When Jesus was a young boy, He grew up with His mother, Mary, and Joseph, who cared for Him. Jesus was kind, obedient, and wise beyond His years.

One time, when Jesus was twelve years old, His family went to Jerusalem for the Feast of Passover. This feast celebrates and calls to remembrance of when I delivered My people from Pharaoh when they were enslaved in Egypt.

Do you remember the story of how I delivered My people, the Israelites, from Pharaoh? Now, through Jesus, I will be delivering My people from all evil powers, from sin and eternal punishment or the place called Hell or the Gehenna.

When it was time to go back home, Mary and Joseph thought Jesus was with their group. But after traveling for a whole day, they realized Jesus was not with them. They hurried back to Jerusalem, looking for Him!

Finally, after three days of worry and misery, they found Him in the temple, sitting with the teachers, listening, and asking questions.

The teachers were amazed at His understanding and correct answers to their questions! Jesus was very wise and smart, and He was merely a young boy. He was wise and smart because He listened to his parents, who had put their trust and faith in Me.

Most importantly, He knew that He was My Unique Son, and so He always listened to Me!

Mary didn't quite understand how I was using Jesus to fulfill Our plan; she, therefore, said to Him, "Son, why have You treated us like this? Your father, Joseph and I have been anxiously searching for You."

Jesus replied, "Why were you searching for Me? Didn't you know I had to be about My Father's business?" You see, Jesus knew that I was His Heavenly Father and that He had a mission or Our plan to accomplish.

Mary and Joseph didn't fully understand, but Jesus went back home to Nazareth with them and continued to grow in wisdom, stature, and favor with both Me, His Father, and man.

You see, this showed that even as a child, Jesus understood His purpose—to do My will and bring and display My kingdom to My people who lived on Earth.

I also want you to perform My will and to be a part of My plan and family to show and tell others about Me, your heavenly Father.

The Twelve Disciples: Jesus' Special Friends

When Jesus grew up and began His ministry, He chose twelve men to be His disciples. They were ordinary people—fishermen, a tax collector, and others.

They didn't have special skills, but they had willing hearts. I chose them because they were humble and willing to learn. I have also chosen you! Will you choose to follow and listen to Me and My Son, Jesus?

Jesus set the perfect example while teaching all of My children and His brothers and sisters, including you, how to pray and how to serve others. Also, how to share the Good News of the spiritual Kingdom of His Father that now belongs to Him.

These twelve disciples and men whom Jesus chose would later become the leaders of My Church after Jesus returned to heaven to be with Me. They will then be called the Twelve Apostles of Jesus.

However, many more people also followed Jesus, including men, women, and even children, who believed in His words and witnessed the miracles He performed.

Do you remember the miracles that I performed through Moses when he was in Egypt? Just like Moses, Jesus also performed miracles or displayed great signs to show the people His Power. Also, to prove that I was with Him and them.

Always remember that Jesus was and is Unique—One of a Kind. And that He performed miracles to prove that He was God, My very Son. Jesus was just like Me, His Father, in every way! He is God! And His Kingdom had come to Earth!

Nicodemus: A Secret Believer

Nicodemus was a religious leader, but he was afraid of the wicked leaders. Therefore, he secretly came to Jesus at night to learn more about My spiritual Kingdom.

Unlike some leaders, called Pharisees, Sadducees and Scribes, who were wicked or spiritually corrupt people, many of whom did not like Jesus because they were prideful and loved to be in power.

Neither did they want to listen to His spiritual teachings about My Kingdom. However, Nicodemus wanted to learn more about My Son, Jesus and Our Spiritual Kingdom.

He was curious and desired to understand how a person could be Born Again. Jesus told him, "You must be born of water and the Spirit." This means that one with a sorrowful heart needs to repent or turn from practicing sinning and confess Jesus as their Lord and Savior.

When this occurs, one is then Born Again, as the Holy Spirit now indwells this believer in Jesus. This results in you now being a part of My Kingdom. Then, you are to live a new life through faith in Jesus, your Great Shepherd and Deliverer.

Though Nicodemus did not fully understand at first, he eventually became a follower of Jesus. Just like Nicodemus, you have to want to know more about My Kingdom so that you can grow in faith or become a spiritually mature child of Mine.

Mary Magdalene: A Life Transformed

Mary Magdalene was once troubled by evil spirits, but she listened to Jesus, and He, therefore, set her free from those bothersome evil spirit beings. Afterward, she became a devoted follower who loved and served Him.

She was one of the first to see Jesus alive after His resurrection when He arose from the dead and the grave. Her story shows that no matter how broken a person's life may be, Jesus can bring healing and restoration.

The Woman at the Well: Living Water

Jesus met a despised or not well-liked Samaritan woman at a well who was there to draw water to drink. However, He offered her Living Water—Himself!

This meant she would spend Eternal Life with Jesus in His Kingdom if only she would put her faith in Him. Or drink of His spiritual Truth and teaching like she would drink water. If she did this, her spirit would no longer thirst. This woman would have everything she need… Jesus!

She had made many mistakes in life, but Jesus did not condemn her. He cared for her, and therefore, He wanted to show the woman just how much He loved her. He revealed that He was the Messiah and her long-awaited King!

She believed in Him! She then told everyone in her town about the arrival of Jesus, their King and Deliverer! This story demonstrates My desire to reach all people, regardless of their past, and offer them Living Water—a new life through Jesus.

Zacchaeus: A Changed Heart

Zacchaeus was a wealthy tax collector known for cheating or stealing from people. The Jewish people, his very own people, really hated him because he was untruthful and took advantage of them.

Because Zacchaeus started feeling bad about how he had treated people. And because he had an empty, lonely heart, when he heard that Jesus was coming to town, he climbed a tree just to see Him.

Jesus noticed Zacchaeus, who was in the tree. He said to him, "Come down," and invited Himself to Zacchaeus' house. After meeting Jesus, Zacchaeus' heart changed! He then promised to give half of his wealth to the poor and repay four times what he had stolen from the people.

This demonstrated that a genuine encounter with Jesus transforms a person's heart and actions. This means that when a person becomes My child, they want to be more like Me, their Father and God. And more like My Son, Jesus.

My children should always be determined to treat people the right way as they show their love, which is My love for others.

Lazarus: A Miracle of Life

Lazarus was a dear friend of Jesus who fell ill and later died. When Jesus arrived, Lazarus had been in the tomb or grave for four days. Jesus wept for His friend, showing His compassion. But then, He called out, "Lazarus, come forth!" and Lazarus came back to life.

This miracle demonstrated that Jesus had and continues to have power over death!

Religious Leaders Who Opposed Jesus

During Jesus' ministry, if you recall, there were some religious leaders who did not like Him. Do you remember what they were called?... Did you remember that they were called the Pharisees, Sadducees, and Scribes?

Even though they were supposed to teach My Word to My people—the Jews, many of these leaders did not truly understand or want to understand My mission. Here's something else about them: Some were even jealous of Jesus because the people followed and worshipped Him.

Neither did these corrupt leaders like that Jesus taught with authority, healed the sick, showed mercy to sinners and said that He was God, My very Son.

Some of them thought they were being faithful to Me. However, they were wrong because they would not listen to My Son, Jesus. Even so, there were others whose hearts were full of pride; subsequently, they were envious of Jesus!

Sadly, Satan, along with demonic or the bad influences of fallen angels, uses people whom I desire to use. However, there are many whose hearts are far from Me to oppose Me and be evil and mean-spirited toward My Son Jesus. This really saddens Me because I love them so much!

You can know about the work of Satan and fallen angels because they often influence people who resist or don't want to listen to My truth. These are people who continuously practice evil or sin.

Likewise, these are people who don't tell the truth because of their stubborn minds or hearts that are sometimes led by evil spirits. But also, their own sinful passions or desires lead these people to rebel against Me and refuse to listen to Jesus and what We teach from the Bible.

These kinds of people oppose or are disobedient towards My goodness or righteousness that I have provided. And so, they refuse to believe in Jesus and what I told Him to say, which is recorded in the Holy Scripture.

But remember, I still love them and want them to be saved, but not everyone will receive Jesus. Not everyone is going to obey Me or listen to what you have to say about Me. This really saddens Me.

I hope that you will always listen to Me and obey what I have to say. Also, you should always pray for those who will not listen to Me. And you should never stop loving such people... the reason why? Because I love them just like I love you... Okay.

Evil Spirits and Demonic Oppression

Now, I need you to really listen to Me carefully! As I've told you plenty of times. There are evil spirits with bad influences. However, they can also make people feel sad, angry, or fearful without any clear reason.

Yes, these evil forces or spirits can oppress people and make them feel very sad or depressed, discouraged, angry and fearful for no reason.

Though My children cannot be possessed by demons because My Spirit lives within them. Nonetheless, some people can be oppressed by these spirits if they are not careful, watchful, prayerful, or such ones who do not read My Word or their Bible.

When people open their lives to evil by watching unholy things or listening to evil or hurtful people. Or, by always doing bad things, they give these wicked spirits a chance to influence them to become really evil and bad people. And even emotionally troubled.

But My children, who put their trust in Me and love Me, have power and authority through the teaching and Power of Jesus. And through the Power of the indwelling Holy Spirit to resist these evil and corrupt spirits and ungodly ways of this world!

Because Jesus is the Lord of lord or Ruler over creation, He even cast out demons from people who were possessed, showing that He is greater and more powerful than all evil spirits, including Satan or the Devil.

Living Water and the Bread of Life

Jesus says in your Bible, "I am the Bread of Life. Whoever comes to Me will never go hungry, and whoever believes in Me will never be thirsty."

Just like your body needs food and water to survive, your spirit always needs Jesus and His teachings through the Holy Spirit to give you a healthy or strong spiritual life that you may live to honor Me.

And, then, one day, when your work on Earth is done, you will live with Me forever in My new Kingdom that is soon to come!

To eat My Bread of Life and to drink My Living Water means to always partake of Jesus and believe in Him and His teaching that you may follow Him, be strengthened in Him and be one with Him.

When you accept Jesus, your spirit will never lack what it needs. This is also because the Holy Spirit has been given to you as your Helper and the Giver of your New Life.

One day, you will live eternally with Me! May your heart be filled with this hope and My love until that great day arrives! That day is coming... I promise!

Miracles That Prove Jesus Is My Son

Jesus performed many miracles to prove His divine authority and power. He healed the blind, raised the dead, cast out demons, and even calmed a very scary and turbulent storm!

Once again, these miracles were signs that My Kingdom had arrived on Earth through My Son, the Messiah, King Jesus! Each miracle Jesus demonstrated proved that I was with Him as He showed that He had power over sickness, death, and all evil forces.

Jesus Reveals My Heart

Jesus came to Earth to confront Satan and all evil powers and to set people free from sin and their evil or bad ways. When you see Jesus at work in the lives of My people, you are seeing My Kingdom breaking through in this evil and broken world.

No matter how bad things look or how bad things may get, remember that I am always with you, that I am always in control and that I have all Power!

Jesus has revealed My heart—a heart full of love, compassion, mercy, and truth. Every miracle performed by Jesus showed My power and My love for My people! There are times that I still work miracles.

However, what's most important to Me is not My miracles but rather that you be full of love, compassion, faith and truth. When you do this, I am well pleased with you, My child.

What You Should Learn and Remember:

1. Jesus reveals My heart—full of love, healing, and forgiveness.
2. Be aware that Satan, along with demonic or bad influences of fallen angels, often tries to hinder those I want to use.
3. Faith in Jesus brings new life and eternal hope.
4. You need spiritual food just like you need physical food—Jesus is your Bread of Life and Living Water.
5. My Kingdom is about healing, forgiveness, and new beginnings.

Memory Verse:

"The Kingdom of God has come near. Repent and believe the Good News!" — Mark 1:15

Let's Talk:

1. What did Jesus preach about God's kingdom?
2. Why did Jesus heal the sick and help people?
3. How did Jesus teach people about God?
4. Who were the apostles and disciples, and what did they do?
5. What made Jesus different from other teachers?
6. How can we follow Jesus in our lives today?

Prayer:

Dear God,

Thank You for sending Jesus to show Your heart.
Help us to believe, follow, and trust in His power.
Thank You for being the Bread of Life and the Living Water.
In Jesus' name, Amen.

CHAPTER 14

The Cross: Jesus Pays the Price for the Sins of the World

(Scripture References: Matthew 27; John 1; Luke 23; Isaiah 53; 2 Corinthians 5:21)

My Dear Children, I will now tell you about the most important act of love in all of history. This is the story of how My Son, Jesus, paid the price for your sins and the sins of the world.

The Plan from the Beginning

Before the Earth was created, My Son, Jesus, had chosen to come to your world as a baby clothed in a human body. We had planned in advance to save you and Our people from what became your fallen world from sin.

Jesus, before the Edenic Fall or when sin entered your world, had pre-determined to pay the horrible cost—pain, suffering, and death through crucifixion for your sins and the sins of the world. His sacrifice would be the greatest display or act of love ever known!

Yes, Jesus loves you!

Do you remember that when Adam and Eve disobeyed Me, corruption and sinfulness entered the entire world? This resulted in My people being separated from Me. Adam's action or inaction resulted in physical and spiritual death for My people and all the living creatures on Earth.

But I promised that one day, someone would come to get rid of sin, corruption, and all evil and to crush Satan or the serpent's head. Well, you already know that this someone was and is My Son, Jesus.

Jesus was sent, and He chose to come to Earth to show My love and to make a way for all people to be forgiven for their sins. His whole life was about doing My will, teaching about My Kingdom, and loving everyone, even those who hated Him.

Jesus Prays in the Garden

Before Jesus was unjustly arrested by those evil leaders who didn't like Him and His teaching, He went to a garden called Gethsemane to pray to Me, His Father. My Son, when He was on Earth, often prayed or talked to Me.

He knew from the very beginning the suffering that was about to happen, and his heart was heavy! So, Jesus prayed, "Father, if it is possible, let this cup or suffering pass from Me. Yet not My will, but Yours be done."

My Son showed complete obedience to Me, even when it was hard. When the soldiers came to arrest Him, one of His disciples, Peter, tried to protect Jesus by swinging his sword and, thereby, cutting off a soldier's ear.

But Jesus healed the man's ear and told Peter to put away his sword. Jesus wanted Peter to know that they were not fighting against people but against the evil spiritual forces of the world.

You must always remember that love, not violence, is Our way to win the battle over evil! When you pray to Me, this shows your reliance on and faith in Me. I will strengthen and lead you when you pray and trust in Me.

This doesn't mean that your life will be without difficulties. However, even as Jesus did, I want you to trust Me and ask that My will be done. Remember that this world's troubles will not always last. One day, and it won't be very long, I am going to make everything new... I promise!

Betrayed and Arrested

One of Jesus' own disciples, Judas Iscariot, because of greed and his wrong heart or way of thinking, betrayed Jesus for thirty pieces of silver. It was Judas who had led the soldiers to the garden, where they arrested My Son.

I was heartbroken! However, because I know what is in the hearts or minds of everyone, Judas' action was part of Our plan to save the world. Jesus accepting the soldier's false arrest of Himself was love in action and obedience toward Me!

The soldiers treated Jesus terribly, hurting Him very badly and mocking or making fun of Him for no reason. Their actions were pure evil!

But what these rebellious people didn't know was that they had also allowed themselves to become influenced by the fallen angels, with Satan as their guiding influence, who wanted to kill Jesus. You see, the people and the evil spirit realm wrongly believed this would stop Our plan.

What these forces of evil did was so unfair! But listen, Jesus remained focused, composed and loving because He knew this was Our plan from the very beginning! Our grand plan of Redemption in order to save Our people from this present evil world!

Often, life in your world is unfair because of sinful people. But just as Jesus did, be strong and follow My will or way no matter the challenges that you will face. If you do this, in the end, you win! You will receive My promises that I have made to you and for the whole of creation!

The Unfair Trials

Jesus was taken to the High Priests, where the people falsely accused Him of doing wrong. The religious leaders were extremely jealous and angry because Jesus said that He was the Son of God.

They didn't truly love or understand Him or Me. Even so, their hearts were filled with envy and pride! Therefore, they handed Jesus over to the Roman governor, Pilate.

Pilate did not find Jesus guilty. Nevertheless, the angry crowd, some were people who once followed Jesus but turned against Him, kept shouting for Jesus to be killed by crucifixion. Pilate sent Jesus to King Herod, but Herod only mocked him and sent him back.

Even though Pilate knew Jesus was innocent, he gave in to the crowd and sentenced Jesus to be crucified. To try and make the people happy, Pilate offered to release one prisoner. The crowd chose a criminal named Barabbas instead of Jesus. They shouted, "Crucify Him!"

Pilate washed his hands to show he didn't want to be responsible, but he still allowed Jesus to be crucified.

My child, you must always remain strong or faithful in and through Me, no matter what! You must not allow evil people to influence you to do wrong! The people of this corrupt and evil world want to do what they want to do. Therefore, they will entice you to join them.

However, to be faithful and strong in Me, My beloved children will remain prayerful, read and study their Bible so that they will know My will and way for their lives. When you do this, you will be victorious over evil... In the end, just like Jesus, you will win!

Mocked and Scorned

The soldiers made fun of Jesus by putting a crown of thorns on His head and dressing Him in a purple robe. They slapped Him, beat Jesus with their fist, spat on him, and pretended to honor My Son as a king to ridicule Him.

They didn't understand or want to believe that Jesus was truly the King of kings and My very own Son! Their actions were the result of their hard hearts that had been corrupted by sin.

After a long night of torture or the beating of Jesus, they then forced Him to carry His heavy wooden Cross through the streets. Upon this Cross, My Son would be crucified. Jesus was so weak from being tortured all night that a man named Simon from Cyrene had to help carry His Cross.

I want you to remember this: just as Simon helped Jesus carry His Cross. I want you to help others when they are going through difficult times. Being loving, kind and helpful is what I require of My children.

The Crucifixion

When they reached the place called Golgotha, where Jesus would give Himself as the Lamb of God, the sacrifice for humanity, they nailed Jesus' hands and feet to the Cross! His suffering on the Cross would be unbearable!

My children, this was Jesus, My Suffering Servant, showing His love for everyone! He chose this pain and suffering so that you may be freed from sin and death!

Above His head, they put a sign that read, "Jesus of Nazareth, King of the Jews." Some people made fun of Him, while others wept or cried.

What the people witnessed and what you are reading about is the ugliness and great cruelty of very evil or sinful people! Even so, the strong influence that the spiritual forces of evil can have on people. As well as how badly the Devil wanted to stop My plan, in his mind, by killing Jesus.

But what the Devil did not know, because he does not know everything. That My Son's sacrifice was Our plan of Salvation for My people and their deliverance from sin and death!

This act of sacrificial love from Jesus has not only brought Salvation to My people. But, through this unprecedented act of grace, My Son's voluntary act of valor led to the crushing of Satan or the serpent's head! That's right; Satan has been defeated!

However, his ultimate end and destruction will soon come! He will be cast into the Gehenna or eternal Hell! I, your God, have made this promise! And it will come to pass!

Two criminals were also crucified next to Jesus. One of them mocked Him, but the other asked Jesus to remember him when He came into His Kingdom. Jesus promised him, "Today you will be with me in paradise."

At that very moment, Jesus forgave this man of his sins; the man became one with Jesus and was granted access and family status into My family and Kingdom!

As Jesus hung on the Cross, He looked at the people who hurt and betrayed Him and prayed, "Father, forgive them, for they do not know what they are doing." This shows Jesus' incredible love and forgiveness, even for those who had hurt and betrayed Him.

Jesus has displayed for you, through His sacrifice and forgiveness, the great love that He has for His people. As My sons and daughters, you too are also to demonstrate such love for all people.

The Women at the Cross

While Jesus hung from the Cross and endured great agony, He saw His mother, Mary and His disciple John standing nearby, full of great sorrow and grief! He made sure they would take care of each other after He was gone.

He said to John, "behold your mother;" to "His mother He said, behold your son." This serves to show how much Jesus loved and cared for his family, even while suffering. Jesus' life clearly demonstrates to you how you are to always do your best to care for others.

The Centurion's Confession

After Jesus gave His life through death by crucifixion, the sky turned dark, and the earth shook! A Roman soldier who had been guarding Jesus saw everything and said, "Surely this man was the Son of God." Even in death, Jesus' love and sacrifice touched people's hearts.

This was Our ultimate plan or strategy: for others to see My love through the suffering of My Son. His suffering became My suffering. Together, We endured the Cross and are now victorious over the work of spiritual wickedness and Satan!

The Significance of the Cross

Jesus' death and Self-sacrifice on the Cross were the most important part of Our plan to save the lost and sinful people of this world. He took the punishment that should have been yours and paid the price for every sin and sinner.

Remember, I loved the world so much that I gave My only Son, Jesus, so that whoever believes in Him will not perish but shall have Eternal Life!

What You Should Learn and Remember:

1. God's Love: Jesus' death on the Cross was the greatest act of love. He died so that our sins could be forgiven.

2. Forgiveness: Even when people were unkind to Him, Jesus forgave them. We should also forgive others.

3. Helping Others: Just like Simon helped Jesus carry His Cross, we should help people when they are going through tough times.

4. Victory over Sin: Jesus' death was not the end — it was the victory over sin and evil.

5. Spiritual Battle: We are not fighting against people but against evil forces. Jesus conquered evil with love and sacrifice; these are your spiritual weapons also.

Memory Verse

"But God demonstrates his own love for us in this: While we were still sinners, Christ died for us." — Romans 5:8 (NIV)

Let's Talk:

1. Why did Jesus have to die on the Cross?
2. What does Jesus' death show us about God's love?
3. How did people treat Jesus before He died?
4. What happened when Jesus died?
5. What does it mean that Jesus paid for our sins?
6. How should we respond to what Jesus did for us?

Prayer:

Dear God,

Thank you for loving me so much that you sent Jesus to die for my sins. Help me to always remember His great sacrifice and to live my life loving others as he did.

Give me the strength to forgive, just like Jesus forgave those who hurt Him.

Teach me to help others carry their burdens, and remind me that love is more powerful than hate.

In Jesus' name, Amen.

CHAPTER 15

The Resurrection: Jesus Defeats Death

(Scripture References: Matthew 24 & 28; Mark 13 &16; Luke 21 & 24; John 20–21; Acts 1:3–11; 1 Corinthians 15:3–8)

My Dear Children,

Now I want to tell you about the most amazing event in history! This is the story of how My Son, Jesus, defeated death and rose from the grave. This moment changed everything, giving hope to everyone who believes in My Son.

Why We Needed a Savior

Remember when Adam and Eve sinned in the Garden of Eden? Because of their disobedience, sin entered the world, and that sin separated all people from Me, their loving Father. Sin brought death, both physical and spiritual.

Since I, your God, am the source of life, being separated from Me meant that all people would die. But I love you so much that I planned a way to rescue you and to bring you back to Me. I sent my Son, Jesus, to defeat sin and death!

Because you believe in Jesus, you are now My sons and daughters. Because Jesus rose from the dead, anyone who believes in Him will also live forever and be reunited with Me in My Eternal Kingdom.

As you already know, after Adam sinned, the world became filled with war, pain, suffering, and death. In the Bible, Matthew Chapter 24, Mark Chapter 13, and Luke Chapter 21, Jesus spoke about how these things would happen on Earth until He returned to make everything right.

When He comes back, He will establish His perfect Kingdom on Earth — that which Adam failed to do. Let Me remind you of My promise: Soon, I will create a New Heaven and Earth where there will be no more pain, sadness, or death, and My children will live with Me forever.

The Sadness After the Cross

After Jesus gave His life on the Cross, His disciples were heartbroken and filled with fear and confusion! They didn't understand that Jesus had to die. They thought He would become a King on Earth and free them from Roman rule and oppression.

During Jesus' crucifixion, some amazing things happened! The sky turned dark, even though it was daytime. The earth shook, and the thick curtain in the temple that separated people from the holy place was torn in two, from top to bottom.

This was My way of showing that through Jesus' sacrifice, anyone could come to Me – the Most Holy God. No longer would My people be separated from Me by sin and death!

After Jesus died, His body was placed in a tomb, and a big stone was rolled in front to seal it. Soldiers guarded the tomb because the religious leaders were afraid that someone might steal His body and claim He was alive.

The disciples didn't know what to do. They had run away into hiding because they were afraid they might be arrested, too.

The Angel Rolls Away the Stone

Early on the first day of the week, while it was still dark, Mary Magdalene went to the tomb. Mary loved Jesus so much and wanted to take care of his body for proper burial. But when she arrived, something amazing had happened!

An angel of the Lord, one of My heavenly servants, had come down from heaven and rolled away the stone! His appearance was like lightning, and his clothes were as white as snow! The guards were so afraid that they shook and fell down like they were dead.

The angel said to the women, "Do not be afraid, for I know that you are looking for Jesus, who was crucified. He is not here; He has risen, just as He said!" This is Good News! And My promise fulfilled.

The Empty Tomb – The Two Disciples Come Running

When Mary saw the empty tomb, she was shocked and ran to tell Peter and John. She said, "They have taken the Lord out of the tomb, and we don't know where they have put Him!"

Peter and John immediately took off running to the tomb. John got there first and looked inside. He saw the strips of linen lying there but didn't go in.

Then Peter arrived and went right into the tomb. He saw the strips of linen and the cloth that had been around Jesus' head folded up by itself. John then went in, too, and when he saw it, he did not understand that Jesus had risen from death and the tomb.

Jesus Appears to Mary Magdalene

After the disciples left, Mary stayed behind, crying. She looked inside the tomb and saw two angels sitting where Jesus' body had been. They asked her why she was crying. Mary said, "They have taken my Lord away!"

Then she turned around and saw someone standing there. It was Jesus, but she didn't recognize Him at first. Jesus asked her, "Why are you crying? Who are you looking for?" Mary thought He was the gardener until He said her name, "Mary." At that moment, she knew it was Jesus!

Mary was overjoyed! Jesus told her to go and tell the disciples that He was alive. Mary ran to share the Good News, saying, "I have seen the Lord!"

Jesus Appears on the Road to Emmaus

That same day, two of Jesus' followers were walking to a village called Emmaus. As they walked, they talked about everything that had happened. Jesus came up and walked with them, but they didn't recognize Him.

He asked what they were discussing, and they told Him about Jesus' death and the empty tomb. Jesus explained how the Scriptures had foretold or prophesied that the Messiah would suffer and then enter His glory. When they reached Emmaus, they invited Jesus to stay with them.

As He broke bread with them, their eyes were opened, and they recognized Jesus! Then, He disappeared from their sight because He had to show Himself to His other disciples or followers.

The disciples excitedly returned to tell the others what had happened!

Jesus Appears to the Disciples

While the two were telling the other disciples about their encounter, Jesus suddenly appeared and stood among them and said, "Peace be with you." The disciples were startled and frightened, thinking they saw a ghost or spirit being!

Jesus reassured them, showing them His hands and feet where the nails had been placed. He even ate a piece of fish to prove He was not a ghost but rather that He still had His physical body. The disciples were filled with joy and amazement!

Thomas's Doubt

One disciple, Thomas, wasn't there when Jesus appeared. When the others told him that Jesus was alive, he didn't believe it. Thomas said, "Unless I see the nail marks and put my finger where the nails were, I will not believe."

A week later, Jesus appeared again while Thomas was with them; He knew Thomas had doubts and questions to be answered. So, Jesus said to Thomas, "Put your finger here and see My hands. Stop doubting and believe." Thomas was amazed and said, "My Lord and My God!"

Jesus told him, "Because you have seen Me, you have believed. Blessed are those who have not seen and yet have believed." This means that you, My child, are blessed through faith because you believe in Me, your Father and My Son, Jesus, whom you have not seen.

This means you have faith in Me because your parents have told you about Me. And this is because they also have faith or have chosen to believe in Me. They have read My Bible, which I have given to the world. You must also learn to do the same thing often… Okay.

Just like Thomas had doubt, sometimes you may have doubt or questions about the Bible or Me. If you should experience this, keep praying, ask Me, your parents and other godly people questions.

But most importantly, always read and study My Word—the Bible, and you will receive answers to your questions! The Holy Spirit who lives in you is going to help you with your questions and lead you to My truths, as provided in the Bible.

If you do this, your faith and understanding will grow or mature. This is what I want to see: you mature spiritually and have great faith in Me, your Father and your Lord, Jesus!

Do you remember what I said about Jesus being your Living Water and the Bread of Life?

Therefore, with great regularity or daily, you need to spend quality time reading and studying from your Bible. When you accomplish this, you are being fed or receiving spiritual nourishment for your soul.

The Holy Spirit is your Helper Who will be your guide to Our truth according to the Bible!

Jesus Appears for Forty Days

After His resurrection, Jesus appeared to His disciples and many others for forty days. He continued to teach them about the Kingdom of God, which is Our Kingdom.

During this time, Jesus was helping His people and Mine understand why He had to die or give His life as a sacrifice for everyone's sin and then rise from the dead.

My Son, Jesus, did this so that you could be cleansed or redeemed from your sins! And then be brought back to Me or restored to My eternal family and Kingdom!

I now say welcome Home!... because you have chosen to believe in My Son, Jesus' teachings and My promises.

Jesus' Ascension

One day, while Jesus was with His disciples, He gave them final instructions to wait in Jerusalem to receive the Holy Spirit. Then, right before their eyes, Jesus was taken up into heaven. A cloud hid Him from their sight.

Currently, My Son Jesus is seated with Me! Very soon, Jesus is going to appear in the sky and call My children to heaven. This is called the Rapture of the Church or My people. Meanwhile, Jesus is awaiting the right time for this to happen.

Then, at His Second Return to Earth, He is going to bring you, along with all of My people, who are also called Saints, to restore or set up His Kingdom on Earth.

When you read your Bible, you will learn that My Son Jesus is also called the second Adam. This is the reason why: He is going to begin to correct all the problems caused by the first Adam's disobedience.

The disciples now knew that Jesus had gone or returned to heaven to be with Me, His Father and yours. But He made a promise that one day, He is going to return to complete His work on Earth!

I have not told anyone when this will happen, but He is coming back! Meanwhile, I want you to always be kind and to show love and compassion to others until My Son and your Lord, Jesus, return for you.

Will you be faithful to honor Me through your living? Are you going to tell people about the Saving Grace of Jesus? I am certain that you will… this is what I require of you.

The Great Commission

Before ascending or returning to His heavenly home, Jesus gave His disciples an important mission.

He said, "Go and make disciples of all nations and all people, baptizing them in the name of the Father, and of the Son, and of the Holy Spirit, teaching them to obey everything I have commanded you. And surely I am with you always, to the very end of the age."

This means that when you have the opportunity to do so, tell others about Jesus' love and His Saving Grace that He offers to all people of this fallen and corrupt world!

What You Should Learn and Remember:

1. Hope and Victory: Jesus defeated death, giving hope to all who believe in Him.
2. Faith Over Doubt: Even when Thomas doubted, Jesus showed love and proof. When you have doubts and questions, pray and seek answers from others while you read and study your Bible.
3. Endurance in Troubles: Jesus warned that there would be hardships, but He promised to return and make things right.
4. Jesus' Continued Presence: Jesus appeared for forty days to teach and strengthen the disciples' faith.
5. Jesus made a promise to send the Holy Spirit, who is also God.
6. Be faithful: One day soon, Jesus is going to return to the sky to Rapture His children.
7. The Promise of a New Heaven and Earth: One day, Jesus will make all things new.
8. The Great Commission: We are called to share Jesus' message of Salvation and deliverance with everyone.
9. Jesus Is Alive: Because Jesus lives, we can have a relationship with Him through the indwelling Holy Spirit and be filled with hope.

Memory Verse

"He is not here; He has risen, just as He said. Come and see the place where He lay." — Matthew 28:6 (NIV)

Let's Talk:

1. What happened on the third day after Jesus died?
2. Who found the empty tomb first?
3. Why is the resurrection important?
4. What does Jesus' victory over death mean for us?
5. How did the disciples react when they saw Jesus alive?
6. What hope does the resurrection give us today?

Prayer:

Dear Father,

Thank you for raising Jesus from the dead and giving us hope.
Help me to believe even when I have doubts and to remember that Jesus, through the indwelling Holy Spirit, is always with me.
Give me the courage to share your love with others.
Thank you for your amazing love.
In Jesus' name, Amen.

CHAPTER 16

Pentecost: God the Holy Spirit Comes to Establish His Church

(Scripture References: Genesis 1:1,2 & 26; Joel 2:28-32; Acts 2:1-4)

My dear Children, before I talk about the amazing day called Pentecost, let's take a moment to recount how it all started:

In Chapter 1, you learned that I created the heavens and the earth. Everything was beautiful and perfect until Adam and Eve disobeyed Me, bringing sin into the world. This sin separated all people from Me, their God. But I made a promise to rescue you through My Son, Jesus.

When Jesus came into the world, He taught about My kingdom, showed love, performed miracles, and ultimately died on the Cross to pay for your sins. Then, three days later, He rose from the dead, defeating sin and death!

Before He returned to Heaven to be with Me, Jesus told His disciples to wait for the Holy Spirit, who would give them power to share the Good News of Jesus with the whole world.

The Trinity at Work – Old Testament and New Testament

I, your God, have always existed as one God in three persons: God the Father, God the Son–Jesus, and God the Holy Spirit. Many have chosen to call this Godhead or Unique Organization the Holy Trinity.

The wording Holy Trinity is not found in the Bible. Nonetheless, you can clearly see the operation of Me your God in three Persons throughout the Bible. Therein, God the Father, Son and Holy Spirit are in view and at work.

I know that Our Uniqueness is a great mystery to you. There may be other things that I may not fully explain in the Bible. However, what's most important is that you repent from practicing sinful ways and accept Jesus as your Lord and Savior.

As for the Holy Spirit, even though He came to indwell believers–My children or the Church during Pentecost, He was already at work long before then. He also eternally exists; He was not created; He is God, one with and equal to Me, the Father and Jesus, My Son.

Together, we can be called the Holy Trinity.

In the Old Testament, you can see the Triune God working together. Genesis 1:1-2 reads, "The Spirit of God was hovering over the waters during creation." "Then God said, Let us make man in Our image" (Genesis 1:26).

The use of the word **"Us"** demonstrates that Me, God the Father, God the Son, and God the Holy Spirit were all involved in creation. So it is, you are made in Our image as spirit beings clothed in a body.

Another example is when I, your God, appeared to Abraham as three men in Genesis 18, a foreshadowing of the mystery of the Trinity. This appearance is a theophany or bodily formation of the Godhead.

If you recall… In the story of Shadrach, Meshach, and Abednego in the fiery furnace (Daniel 3), a fourth figure is seen appearing with them — "one who looks like a son of the gods. This is a pre-incarnate or Christophany appearance of Jesus.

In Psalm 110:1, King David says, "The Lord says to my Lord: 'Sit at my right hand until I make your enemies a footstool for your feet.'" This verse shows a conversation between Me, God the Father and God the Son, revealing the relationship within the Trinity.

Therefore, when you read in your Bible the Holy Spirit's coming at Pentecost, it is not a new arrival. But rather a new way of God, the Holy Spirit, being with you and indwelling you when My Son Jesus returns to His heavenly home to be with Me.

So it is; I'm always with you and My beloved children.

The Promise of the Holy Spirit

After Jesus returned to heaven, His disciples did exactly what He told them to do — they waited and prayed together in one place. They were in an upstairs room in Jerusalem, all united in their prayers and hopes.

They didn't know exactly what would happen, but they trusted Jesus' promise that the Holy Spirit would come. One day, as they were gathered, something incredible took place!

Suddenly, there was a sound like a mighty rushing wind that filled the whole house! Then, they saw what looked like tongues of fire that came to rest on each of them. This was the Holy Spirit, coming to live inside or indwell My children just as Jesus had promised!

Jesus, God the Son, had walked among His people. Now, God the Holy Spirit would indwell and infill or empower His people—believers in Jesus throughout the entire world to live for Me, their God!

Speaking in Tongues – The Miracle of Languages

When the Holy Spirit indwelled and then infilled or empowered the disciples of Jesus, they began to speak in other tongues or languages that they had never learned before. This was also a miracle or supernatural act that I performed upon My children.

God, the Holy Spirit, had given Our people the ability to speak in real languages so that people from all over the world could hear the message of Jesus in their own language.

This was an important moment because it showed that the Good News of Jesus was for everyone, no matter where they were from or what language they spoke.

You see, a long time ago, as shared in the Old Testament, people tried to build a huge tower called Babel to reach heaven without Me, their God. They were prideful and disobedient people, so I confused their languages and scattered them all over the earth (Genesis 11).

But now, God, the Holy Spirit, was doing something new! He was uniting people by allowing them to hear the message or Good News of Jesus in their own language.

Boldness Through the Holy Spirit – Peter's Transformation

One of the most amazing changes happened to Peter! Before, Peter had been afraid to even admit he knew Jesus when Jesus was arrested.

But now, having seen Jesus alive and with the Holy Spirit living in him, Peter became bold and fearless! He stood up in front of a huge crowd and preached about Jesus!

Peter explained that Jesus was the Messiah who had been killed but was now alive! He reminded the people that God, long ago, had already promised through the prophet Joel that the Holy Spirit would come to make great things happen with His people.

He reminded the people what Joel had said: "And afterward, I will pour out my Spirit on all people. Your sons and daughters will prophesy, your old men will dream dreams, your young men will see visions." — Joel 2:28

Peter spoke with such confidence and power that people were amazed! They knew Peter was just an ordinary man, but they realized that I was working through him. That's what the Holy Spirit does — He empowers ordinary people to do extraordinary things for the Kingdom of your God.

The First Sermon and the Birth of the Church

Peter's message touched the hearts of the people. They asked, "What should we do?" Peter told them to repent or turn away from sin and be baptized in the name of Jesus for the forgiveness of their sins. He promised that they would also receive the Holy Spirit.

That day, about 3,000 people believed in Jesus and were baptized! This was the beginning of the Christian Church!

The Power of the Holy Spirit

The Holy Spirit gave the disciples courage, wisdom, and the ability to perform miracles! The disciples spoke boldly about Jesus, even when some leaders tried to stop them.

People noticed that these were ordinary men who had been transformed by being with Jesus and being filled with the Holy Spirit (Acts 4:13).

What You Should Learn and Remember:

1. God Keeps His Promises: Jesus promised the Holy Spirit would come, and He did.
2. The Holy Spirit Empowers Us: Just as Peter became brave, the Holy Spirit helps us share God's love.
3. God Loves All People: The gift of speaking in different languages shows that the message of Jesus is for everyone.
4. God Works Through Ordinary People: The Holy Spirit helps believers do great things, just like the disciples.
5. Unity in the Spirit: God brought people together on Pentecost, showing that His love is for all nations or all people.
6. One God in Three Persons: The Father, the Son, and the Holy Spirit work together in perfect unity, as seen in both the Old and New Testaments.

Memory Verse:

"But you will receive power when the Holy Spirit comes on you, and you will be my witnesses in Jerusalem, and in all Judea and Samaria, and to the ends of the earth." — Acts 1:8 (NIV)

Let's Talk:

1. Who was praying together in the upper room?
2. What sound filled the room when the Holy Spirit came?
3. What did the people begin to do after receiving the Holy Spirit?
4. Why did God give the Holy Spirit to the believers?
5. How did Peter change after being filled with the Holy Spirit?
6. How does the Holy Spirit help us today?

Prayer:

Dear God,

Thank you for sending the Holy Spirit to live in us and help us follow you.

Please empower us with your Spirit so we can be bold like Peter and share your love with others.

Help us remember that your message is for everyone.

Thank you for making us a part of your family.

In Jesus' name, Amen.

CHAPTER 17

The Work of the Holy Spirit and the Church: Spreading the Gospel

Scripture References:

- Acts 9 — The Conversion of Saul
- Acts 16 — Paul and Silas in Prison
- Romans 12 — Living Sacrifices and Humble Service
- 1 Corinthians 1 — Unity and the Power of the Cross
- Galatians 3:28 — Unity in Christ
- Epistles Overview — Romans to Jude

My beloved children, now that you have learned about how the Holy Spirit came at Pentecost, indwelled and infilled the early Church, giving My children the power to share the Good News of Jesus.

I will now show you how the Holy Spirit continued to work through the apostles and disciples to spread the gospel to the world. The Book of Acts tells us about the birth of the Church—My body of believers and how the Holy Spirit guided them.

Through the preaching and teaching of the apostles and disciples of Jesus, the gospel spread throughout the known world. It was shared in new places, new cultures, and even people who were once considered enemies of My people and Me.

The Gospel Crosses Boundaries

At first, the early believers mainly shared the message of Jesus with other Jews. But soon, the Holy Spirit made it clear that the Gospel or Good News of Jesus was for everyone — Jews and non-Jews or Gentiles alike.

This – the conversion of Jewish people and Gentile people to Christianity was something that many of the early Jewish people had a hard time understanding. However, the Holy Spirit showed them that Jesus came to break down the divisive walls that separated people.

The twelve apostles preached the Good News to people from different cultures, languages, and religions. The church grew and crossed territorial boundaries, religious boundaries, ethnic boundaries, and cultural boundaries.

In Christ, all people who have rejected sin and the corrupt teachings of this world are equal and are called to unity and love (Galatians 3:28).

The Courageous Preaching of Stephen — The First Martyr

One of the first leaders in the early church was Stephen, a Deacon and man full of faith and the Holy Spirit. Stephen was chosen to help care for the needs of the church members, but he also boldly preached about Jesus.

His powerful words angered some religious leaders who did not believe in Jesus, and they falsely accused him, just like they did to Jesus. Stephen was brought before the Sanhedrin, the Jewish council, for questioning. And instead of defending himself, he boldly spoke the truth about Jesus.

As Stephen proclaimed that Jesus was the Righteous One sent from God, the crowd became furious! They took Stephen outside the city and stoned him to death!

As he was dying, Stephen prayed, "Lord, do not hold this sin against them," just as Jesus had prayed for His enemies while He hung nailed to the Cross. (See Acts 7:60).

Stephen became the first martyr, meaning someone who died for their faith in the early Church. His death showed the courage and faith that believers could have through the power of the Holy Spirit.

Persecution and Spiritual Wickedness

My child, it's important to remember that when people hurt you or others, it shows that their hearts are sinful. I have also told you that such people can also be influenced by spiritual wickedness from other people.

Even so, such negative or bad acts can also involve the influence of the fallen or wicked angels. However, the Devil himself prefers to target or influence people in great leadership positions. Therefore, such people in positions of power and influence he targets to further his corruption.

This is why I have informed you that you are not fighting against other people but against spiritual forces of evil (Eph. 6:12). So, remember, Satan and his fallen angels plan is to use people to do evil things and keep them from knowing My truth or to turn them away from Me.

With that being said, as My children, you are called to love your enemies and pray for those who hurt you. When you have the opportunity, you should even do good for them. This is how you show the world the love of Jesus and that you are one with Him.

Saul Becomes Paul – A Great Missionary

One of the people who witnessed Stephen's death was a young man named Saul. Saul was a Pharisee who hated Christians and wanted to destroy My Church. He even got permission from religious leaders to arrest those who believed in My Son, Jesus.

But I had other plans for Saul. One day, as Saul was traveling to a city called Damascus to arrest Christians, I caused a bright light from heaven to flash around him, and he fell to the ground! A voice said, "Saul, Saul, why do you persecute Me?" This was My Son Jesus, who was speaking.

Saul was blinded by the light and led into the city. I sent a believer named Ananias to heal Saul and explain that he had been chosen to share the gospel with Gentiles and kings. Saul was baptized and became known as Paul.

Once a fierce enemy of Christians, Paul became one of the greatest missionaries in Church history, traveling far and wide to share the Good News of Jesus!

Paul's Trials and Boldness

Paul faced many challenges as he spread the Gospel or Good News of Jesus. Once, while in prison for preaching, Paul and his friend Silas were singing and praying to God. Even though they were chained and mistreated, they praised God!

Suddenly, there was an earthquake, and the prison doors flew open! The jailer, thinking the prisoners had escaped, was about to kill himself. But Paul called out, "We are all here!"

The jailer, amazed by their faith, asked, "What must I do to be saved?" Paul replied, "Believe in the Lord Jesus, and you will be saved." That night, the jailer and his whole family became believers in Jesus!

This story is to remind you that even in difficult times, you must keep praising Me, your God and never lose faith. I can turn your hardships into testimonies that touch others' lives.

A Church That Perseveres

The early church faced persecution, hardship, and even death or martyrdom, but they continued to share the Gospel with boldness and love.

Even today, Christians around the world continue to spread the Good News. Sometimes at great personal cost, and many have become martyrs, just like Stephen and many others throughout history.

The Church—My body of believers has endured for over 2,000 years. Even when bad things happen to good people or when natural disasters trouble your world, I, your God, am still in control.

And so, I promise to one day and for all eternity to bless you and fulfill My promises!

What You Should Learn and Remember:

1. The Gospel Unites: Through Jesus, all people can become one family in God.
2. God Can Change Lives: Saul became Paul — from persecutor to preacher.
3. The Holy Spirit Gives Boldness: Ordinary people did amazing things through God's Power.
4. The Church Endures: Despite persecution, the Church continues to grow and thrive.
5. Praise God in Hard Times: Like Paul, you should sing and pray even when facing challenges.
6. Love Your Enemies: Pray for those who hurt you because spiritual wickedness may be influencing them. And this is the will of God: to save all people.

Memory Verse

"For we do not wrestle against flesh and blood, but against the rulers, against the authorities, against the cosmic powers over this present darkness." — Ephesians 6:12 (ESV)

Let's Talk:

1. Who helped the early Church spread the gospel?
2. What happened to Stephen for preaching about Jesus?

3. Who was Saul, and how did he become Paul?
4. How did the Holy Spirit guide the apostles?
5. What does it mean that the Church is the body of believers?
6. How can we share the gospel like the early Church did?

Prayer:

Dear God,

Thank you for the gift of your Holy Spirit and for the courage you give us to stand strong in our faith. Help us to remember that when people hurt us, they may be influenced by evil forces.

Help us to love and pray for our enemies just like Jesus did. Give us the boldness to praise you even in tough times and to always share the Good News of Jesus.

In His name, Amen.

CHAPTER 18

New Creation: God Makes All Things New

Scripture References:

- **Revelation 1 — Jesus Reveals the Future**
- **Revelation 21:1-4 — A New Heaven and a New Earth**
- **Revelation 22:1-5 — The River of Life**
- **Isaiah 65:17 — New Heavens and a New Earth**
- **2 Peter 3:13 — The Promise of a New Creation**

My children, we have come to the final chapter of My story according to the Bible, as recorded in the Book of Revelation. Here, you will learn about the restoration of My Kingdom on Earth. And, lastly, Me creating the New Heaven and Earth!

It is full of amazing visions, promises, warnings, and the final victory of Jesus – the Lion of Judah and King of kings, over all evil principalities and powers!

This amazing book gives us a glimpse of the future and shows us how I, your God, and Jesus My Son, through the Power of the Holy Spirit, will make all things new!

The Book of Revelation is special because it summarizes the entire Bible. It shows how Jesus will make everything new and perfect in the end. However, some parts of My Book of Revelation are mysterious, which means they can be difficult to understand.

Nevertheless, My mysteries, as seen throughout the Bible, and particularly in the Book of Revelation, are hidden truths you can only understand when you read the whole Bible and gain spiritual understanding.

That said, you really must have a very good understanding of certain books in the Old Testament before you can begin to understand the Book of Revelation.

This Book of Revelation uses symbols and words that remind you of stories from the Old Testament.

Therefore, it's very important for you to be familiar with both the Old Testament and New Testament in order that you may begin to comprehend My mysteries—hidden truths of My final plan for the End of Days.

My Revelation or Revealings to John

The Book of Revelation opens with John, one of Jesus' disciples, who was exiled to the island of Patmos for preaching about Jesus. On this island, John was imprisoned or persecuted for his faith in Jesus.

However, while he was on the island, Jesus appeared to John in a vision to give him reassurance of His promises for the future.

Jesus showed John amazing things that would happen during the End of Days and gave him messages for seven churches. These messages encouraged believers and My people today to stay faithful even when facing hardship.

Messages to the Seven Churches

Jesus, through the letters He told John to write, spoke to the seven churches and encouraged them to keep their faith and follow Him even when it was hard. He warned them about false teachings, lukewarm faith, and falling away from His teachings.

These seven letters are to remind you that, as believers in Jesus the Christ, you must stay strong, remain faithful, and continue to love My Son Jesus no matter what!

The Final Battle and God's Judgment

Jesus revealed to John that one day, at His Second Coming, He would return to judge the world. He will then punish all wicked spirits–human beings, including Satan and his fallen angels.

Every person who continues to practice evil and who rejects Me and My Son will be eternally punished!

My coming judgments or wrath or The Great Tribulations that are seen in the Book of Revelation are not to scare you. But instead, to show the world that I am Holy, a Just God. And that I will right the wrongs caused by sin and the evil spiritual powers!

However, people who refuse to follow Jesus and choose wickedness over My love and truth will face My eternal judgment. This is because I must judge sin and get rid of wickedness before I make all things new.

Those who love My Son Jesus and follow Him will not face My wrath or punishment. Instead, they will celebrate when Jesus comes back to Earth with them at His Second Coming to establish His Kingdom!

Remember that I told you that My children or Church will be Raptured or caught up to meet with Jesus in the air? Therefore, those who belong to Jesus will not experience My Great Wrath that is coming upon Earth to judge all who are wicked.

During this time, you and all My children will be with Me in Heaven. After I punish all the wicked-rebellious ones, then Jesus will establish His Kingdom on Earth.

The Return of Jesus -- His Second Coming

After I judge evil, Jesus will return to earth as King of kings. He will defeat the forces of evil once and for all! However, Satan, for 1,000 years, will be cast into the pit, a dark prison I made especially for Him and the really wicked fallen angels.

During this time, Jesus will establish His kingdom on Earth for a millennium or 1,000 years. While Jesus reigns and rules as My King, there will be peace, righteousness, and joy on Earth! Jesus will right the wrongs and correct and perfect that which Adam failed to do.

After the 1,000 years are completed, I will release Satan from the abyss or his prison. This is when Jesus will finally crush the head or deal with Satan. At this time, Jesus will also justly punish all the other remaining people on Earth who chose not to follow and obey Him as King and Lord.

Sin and evil will be no more! Jesus will accomplish His victory by only speaking His Word!

Then, Satan and these new rebellious people will be defeated forever! After which, I will create My New Heaven and the New Earth. This old world, with all its pain, suffering, and sin, will pass away!

A New Heaven and a New Earth

John saw a vision of the New Heaven and New Earth. He saw the New Jerusalem coming down from heaven, a beautiful city where Jesus will forever live with His people.

There will be no more tears, no more death, and no more pain (Revelation 21:4). I, their God and yours will wipe away every tear, and then each of you will live with My Son, Jesus, for eternity!

There will be a River of Life flowing from My throne, and the Trees of Life will bear fruit and bring healing to the nations or all of My children (Revelation 22:1-2). My people will reign with My Son Jesus and serve Him joyfully forever and ever!

The Great Hope

It's important that I remind you this one last time: that it was because of the sins of Adam and Eve that you became separated from Me, the God who gives Eternal Life.

Sin had brought death into the world. However, Jesus came to Earth to defeat both sin and death and take away your sinful condition!

Now that Jesus has conquered death, at My appointed time, when He appears in the sky. You who have believed in Him, at your death, will also be raised or resurrected from the dead, as it was with Jesus, but now, to meet Him in the air.

As for those who are alive and who remained faithful to Jesus, when He appears in the air will also be Raptured to the sky to live with Jesus forever! You will be reunited with Me, your God and Father, eternally or forever in My Kingdom!

Reminder of The Great Commission

Here's another final and very important reminder: Before Jesus ascended and returned to heaven, He gave His disciples a mission:

He said, "Go therefore and make disciples of all nations or all people, baptizing them in the name of the Father and of the Son and of the Holy Spirit" (Matthew 28:19). This is called the Great Commission.

My children, while you remain on Earth, be sure to share the Good News of Jesus with everyone! Please tell My people about the love and Salvation offered through My Son and your Lord and Savior, Jesus.

What You Should Learn and Remember:

1. God Wins: Despite the present evil and suffering, God is going to make all things right!
2. Jesus is King: He will return to Earth, defeat evil, and establish His kingdom.
3. A New Beginning: God will create a New Heaven and a New Earth where sin and death will no longer exist.
4. Hope for Believers: Those who love and follow Jesus will live with Him forever.
5. The Great Commission: We must share the Good News of Jesus with all nations or all people.

Memory Verse

"He will wipe every tear from their eyes. There will be no more death or mourning or crying or pain, for the old order of things has passed away."
— Revelation 21:4 (NIV)

Let's Talk

1. Who gave John the visions in Revelation?
2. What did Jesus tell John to share with the churches?
3. What will happen to evil and sin in the end?
4. What is the New Heaven and New Earth?
5. How can we be ready for Jesus' return?
6. What does it mean to live with God forever?

Prayer:

Dear Daddy,

Thank you for the promise of a new creation and for sending Jesus to defeat death and take away our sins. Help us to live in hope and share Your love with others, just as You commanded.
Remind us that no matter what happens, You are in control and will make all things new.
Thank you for the promise that one day, we will live with You forever.
In Jesus' name, I pray, Amen.

My children, you have learned a lot about Me, your Father,
My Son, Jesus and the Holy Spirit! I am so proud of you!

However, there is so much more I want you to learn that has not been
shared in this book's Bible overview provided by My child, Tony.

As soon as you are able, I want you to begin reading from your
personal Bible that I have provided to the entire world.

I look forward to continuing to talk to you from
My perfect and complete Word—the Bible.

Message from the Author, Tony Scott

My beloved grandchildren and generations to come, my sons and daughters and sisters and brothers in the faith of Jesus,

You have journeyed through some of the most amazing stories ever told. They are God's stories, showing the love He has for His people.

From the beginning, when God made the world and placed Adam and Eve in the Garden of Eden, to the end, where God promises a New Heaven and a New Earth, we have seen how much God loves us and how He never gives up on His people.

The Bible tells us about the problem of sin and how it separates us from God our Father. But God made a way to bring us back to His family through Jesus the Christ.

Jesus came to rescue us by living a perfect life, dying on the Cross for our sins, and rising from the dead. Because of His great sacrifice, we can be forgiven and reconciled to God, our Father.

You also learned about the Holy Spirit, who lives in everyone who believes in Jesus. The Spirit gives us strength, guidance, and courage to live for God, just like the disciples did after Jesus ascended to heaven.

As you grow spiritually in Jesus, remember that God, our Father, loves you, and His plan for your life is good. Keep reading the Bible, praying, and following Jesus. Never forget that you are part of God's big story. Share His love with others and be a light in the world.

One day, Jesus will come back to make all things new, and we will live with Him forever in a perfect world with no pain, no sadness, and no death. Until then, let's keep our eyes on Jesus and live in a way that honors Him.

Epilogue

As the story of God's love comes to a close, it's important to remember that this is not really the end. The Bible is more than just a story — it's the living Word of God. It's a message of hope, love, and Salvation that continues to impact lives today.

The apostles and early believers spread the Good News of Jesus to the world despite persecution, hardship, and sacrifice. Their courage shows us that following Jesus isn't always easy, but it's always worth it. They knew that Jesus was worth everything because He gave His life for us.

You, too, are part of this ongoing story. When you choose to follow Jesus, you join the great family of God that spans generations and nations. You become part of God's mission to share His love and truth with everyone.

Your journey with God doesn't end when you close this book. It continues every day as you grow in faith, learn more about Jesus, and share His love with others. You are called to be light in the world, showing others the way to God through your words, actions, and faith.

Always remember that God is with you, guiding you through the Holy Spirit. When challenges come, know that God is faithful. One day, all the pain and struggles of this world will be gone, and we will live with God forever in His perfect kingdom.

Until then, keep your heart focused on Jesus. Live out your faith boldly, love others deeply, and never lose hope. The best is yet to come!

www.ingramcontent.com/pod-product-compliance
Lightning Source LLC
Chambersburg PA
CBHW050221270326
41914CB00003BA/519